Dorothy Hammond Innes

WHAT LANDS ARE THESE?

Drawings by
CAVENDISH MORTON

Fontana/Collins

First published in Great Britain by
William Collins and Harvill Press 1981
First issued in Fontana Paperbacks 1983

Copyright © Dorothy Hammond Innes 1981

Made and printed in Great Britain by
William Collins Sons & Co. Ltd, Glasgow

The author would like to express her appreciation
for permission to reprint 'Christmas of the Lioness',
written for *Harpers & Queen*.

The extract from *A Shropshire Lad* by A. E. Housman
is reproduced by permission of The Society of Authors as
the literary representative of the Estate of A. E. Housman,
and Jonathan Cape Ltd, publishers of
A. E. Housman's *Collected Poems*.

To my Mother
who always used to hope
I would write a book some day

Contents

Introduction

I thought of calling this book *Where the Pathways Cease*, but feared it might sound presumptuous. Yet that is the link between these four records. In the bush of northern Kenya, in the highlands of Papua New Guinea, in Pakistan (that tapestry of contrasts!) and also in the Welsh hills where we have restored an old hill farm, I felt very strongly that in leaving the road we were entering a secret and different world, still complete in itself.

I described my first book, *Occasions*, as 'verbal photographs of things I want to remember'. Since then we have made wonderful journeys in Africa which resulted in my husband's novel, *The Big Footprints*, and a pilgrimage through Papua New Guinea which led to *Solomon's Seal*. Most recently, we have explored Pakistan.

Finally, after the umbrella-shaped acacia trees which are the signature of East Africa, the clouded bulky mountains of P.N.G., and the kaleidoscope of Pakistan, I have set Wales. Partly because the balance of our lives is to lose ourselves in some strange country till we have forgotten any other place, and then to come back, always to come back to our own country; but chiefly because Wales, too, is another race, another language, another beauty.

But nothing stays the same. These places too will ultimately be stirred into a uniformity of food, clothes, and behaviour. I am lucky to have seen them first. That is what I want to remember. That is what I have tried to pass on.

Part I

AFRICA

Christmas of the Lioness

CHRISTMAS SHOULD BE either one's own home, lit with candles, trimmed with evergreen, filled with one's friends eating and drinking; or it should be something remote and strange.

We were very honoured when George Adamson, hearing we were coming to Kenya, invited us to spend Christmas with him at his permanent camp on the Tana River in the Northern Frontier District. This legendary man doesn't bother much with humans, and has the reputation of not wanting humans to bother him.

We met Joy Adamson in a Cessna on a landing strip near her home on Lake Naivasha. She had filled it with Christmas fare, including a Christmas tree flown out to her from Austria, and suggested we jettisoned our luggage. As we were going on our own

13

safari when we left George, and had left everything we didn't need in Nairobi, we clung stubbornly to our few bits. The pilot said, 'You know Cessnas! If you can get them off the ground, they'll fly!' He did get it off the ground, though Joy had to ride with the Christmas tree on her lap.

To me the low-flying journey over unknown forests and lakes and bush, between unknown hills to an unknown destination, had the magic which people who're good at geography and understand where they're going, can never know. After about an hour and a half we went down on to a cleared patch in the bush, and George Adamson, looking like a lion or like an Old Testament prophet, with his magnificent head, hair and beard, was waiting for us in the shade of an acacia tree beside his Land Rover.

The heat hit us. 'Kora is a particular heat trap, it seems to lie here,' they said. We all had a cool drink, said goodbye to our pilot, arranging for him to come back for us on a certain day, and waved off the Cessna.

George Adamson drives his Land Rover along a bush track with his head out at the side, reading the footprints like a map. Part of the way back to his camp lay beside the Tana River, wide, with the peaceful fat snouts of a family of hippopotamus breaking the surface like a group of rocks. The livid green line in the water near them was a crocodile's back.

My husband, Ralph, who generally sees things with the naked eye before other people see them with binoculars, suddenly said, 'Isn't that an elephant – on the other side of the river, under that clump of trees that come right down to the water?' 'No-o!' said Joy. 'It's a rock.' Then it came down slowly to the river and drank.

Is it a little unreal, this first glimpse of something whose look is so familiar, realising that he is free, his own master in his natural world? No, I don't think so. From that first hour in the African bush, I was overwhelmingly conscious that we were intruders in a very strong world, complete in itself, which has endured with little change through all the ages of man's habitation on earth and long before.

A scatter of parked Land Rovers showed we had arrived. George's African servants stood smiling beside the gate in the wire fence which he had – reluctantly – been persuaded to put round his camp. Four or five large huts grouped round the central mess tent, the communal living room. These *bandas* are built with a thick thatch of palm on a base of chicken-wire, open-sided, so that any air can stir through them. Inside, cords are strung to hang one's clothes, and canvas pockets slung between the posts of the walls to keep things in. Two camp beds with tables beside them, on each a powerful torch, our equipment when the black velvet night falls so suddenly. Close to the camp, rather dominating it so that one is always conscious of them as a part of one's home, are three very red rocks – an unusual eruption in this area, so myth and legend have always gathered round them.

Days fell into a pattern dictated by the heat. Early breakfast, then out with George in the Land Rover. He had made these paths through the bush, just as in other parts of the N.F.D. he had made the original tracks which are now roads. His elder brother, Terence, who now shares this camp, is an engineer, and had done much of the early roading in Kenya. They are very much the story of this part of Africa, these two redoubtable old men – 'old' in the African sense, meaning wise and worthy of honour.

By the time we got back to camp, the day's heat had become too heavy a burden, and for a few hours nothing stirred, neither black, white, nor animal. After a light lunch and a cold drink we all crept off to our huts to lie on our beds with our heads in the centre of the room, to catch the first freshness of the air. After a few hours the general torpor was broken by faint stirrings. Life was beginning again. We rose to the forgiving evening, and set out again in the Land Rover, watching always for the two dik-diks, the enchanting smallest of the antelope species, minute, delicate, wary, crossing the path ahead, first one and then the other, 'always watch for the second, if one is alone, the other must have been killed.' When we got back to camp, darkness fell with astonishing suddenness. There was a brief moment when you could see across the camp, see the Africans hurrying about with buckets of hot water for the showers. The shower was a canvas bucket fixed in a tree above a narrow canvas screen; you pulled a string and the water fell deliciously over you. I loved standing in the hot shower looking up through the branches of the tree to watch the stars come out, yellow and close in the black plush sky. This is the time of day I remember with most delight; the figures of the Africans in silhouette around the cooking fire, and delicious smells creeping towards us. Walking from my hut with a torch shining on the ground ahead to save me falling over ropes and boxes, guided by voices to join the others, sitting over drinks in the dark. We were six people; Joy and George and Terence and their game warden friend, Ken Smith, who had come for Christmas (and brought me a string of yellow amber-like beads much prized among the Northern tribes, which I am wearing as I write).

George would metamorphosise out of invisibility and pour me a drink, then from time to time as we talked, he would raise his torch and sweep a powerful beam of light across the wire a few feet away; and outside our enclosure, free of all Africa, a lion head would turn towards us, blinking in the light, and you could just make out the sinuous tawny bodies before the light switched off.

There were three lions around the camp at that time. Two young lionesses, Liza and Juma, both of whom had recently had their first litters, and the lion Christian – who was not, they thought, the father of either litter, though he had indeed become a real lion (rescued from a London pet store by two young men who ran an antique shop in Chelsea, then, by their wish, brought out here by Bill Travers). He had fought a long war with a local lion, and finally managed to establish his right to the area extending from the camp, and was thought to have mated with another lioness.

Dinner was announced by the beautiful African who put on a vivid coloured *kikoy* for the evening, and he lit a dazzling white Tilley lamp above the table in the mess tent. The contrast was violent after the black night and the blazing stars. It also attracted innumerable tiny green insects which got into the soup. They looked quite pretty, and there was nothing to do but regard them as a garnish. It was over the green-speckled soup, I remember, that I asked George the real meaning of the word 'Safari', now so cheapened and ludicrously abused. He told me it was a Swahili word with Arab connotations, and meant 'the journey of a day'; as far as you can travel between one night's camp and the next night's camp – the traditional and still the best way of moving about Africa. George had a good cook, and round that table, I realised, were three men who each had extraordinary experience, knowledge and understanding of Kenya, the essential and enduring Kenya, as well as a shrewd knowledge and close contact with the waves passing over it now. I asked and they answered. Wonderfully satisfying meals!

I went to sleep to Christian's roaring just behind my head, but I don't think 'roaring' describes a lion's voice at all. I heard him dragging the noise up from the end of his paws and drawing it through his whole body, till at last it poured out in a long reverberating sound that seemed to go on for ever, and died away reluctantly. It is not aggressive. It is an announcement. It says, 'I am the lion of this place. I am here. This is mine.'

On Christmas Eve, George wanted to visit Liza. A lioness moves her cubs every few days, sometimes making difficult journeys over steep country, going back and forth to carry each cub in her mouth, even when they have become heavy. He thought he knew where she was. He said we could come with him and wait in the Land Rover while he went to look for her.

We drove through a part of the bush I hadn't seen, and at last George stopped the Land Rover. 'If I find her, it might be possible for you to come and see her and the cubs, if you'd like. I'll see what mood she's in, if she's relaxed and quiet. Wait here.' After about twenty minutes he came back through the trees, and a few paces behind him Liza came into view, following like a dog, sinuous and sleek and golden. She gave us a calm, thoughtful look, then turned away and disappeared into the bush. She was at camp before us, I think, cutting through the trees while we had to take the track.

In the mess tent that night, Joy had hung her Christmas decorations, familiar and touching, because I had seen them in the photograph of their Christmas camp at the end of her book *Born Free*. Always she hangs this tinsel and places these little candles in some dark jungle clearing to make her lit moment of Christmas, and this year there was her precious Austrian Christmas tree as a centrepiece. We exchanged our presents before dinner, and drank champagne. The turkey was enormous. George said it was a turkey – it's the only time I have ever doubted anything he told me. Anyhow, it was very good, and a (tinned) Christmas pudding was delicious.

The next day after tea, George again wanted to visit Liza, sensing she was on the move and not wanting to lose touch with her. The other young lioness, Juma, though she visited the camp, was more secret and he left her alone. These two were both 'wild' lionesses, born in the bush and not, like Christian, saved by men of imagination from the slow atrophy of parks and zoos.

George left the Land Rover in the same place as the previous day. 'If I don't come back in about quarter of an hour, come after me. It'll mean she's relaxed and won't mind you. Send Dorothy first.' He didn't come back, and I followed him, fascinated but slightly frightened. I didn't know how far he'd gone. I came upon him suddenly, standing very still and looking fixedly towards some bushes. I stopped beside him and followed his glance. At first I couldn't see anything but the pattern of leaves and twigs. Then I saw movement – her pink tongue rhythmically licking three very small cubs clambering over her forepaws. She was about fifteen feet away, looking straight at me with amber eyes, an intelligent, perfectly aware look. My scent was probably familiar to her from the camp, but of course it was George's presence that reassured her. From time to time he spoke to her, a quiet sound with which she had become familiar, 'Liz-za . . . Liz-za.' He turned to me and I remember his brilliant blue eyes were alight with pleasure and pride; 'It's a wonderful example of confidence, isn't it?'

Later, I was to see many wild animals very close – elephants, even a black rhino, Cape buffalo; Hugo van Lawick's wild dogs sniffing all round our car; another lioness with cubs in the Serengeti. But then I would be in a Range Rover, insulated, merely a spectator... Now we were far from our vehicle, and this animal was perfectly conscious of us and kept her eyes on us, yet the rhythm of her tongue licking the cubs never wavered. This was a meeting, person accepting person, not just a viewing. First Ralph, a moment later Joy, finally Ken quietly joined us. Liza stopped licking, rolled over on to her side, and began suckling.

Thoughts flickered to me in that quiet moment in another world. I'd seen George slip a revolver into his belt before we left the Land Rover. A necessary precaution, but how appalling to think of his having to shoot his darling because some idiot visitor behaved thoughtlessly. I remembered this was Christmas Day, and the image of Christmas is a mother and child. This year's mother lay sprawled contentedly under bushes feeding her young. It would take her two years to raise and train them, teaching them all they needed to become independent. Two years of hard work before she was free to mate and start all over again.

We slipped away one by one and she watched us go. Later that night she came to camp.

A few months later, back in England, we heard Liza was dead, and Juma had adopted her cubs and was making a desperate effort to raise both families, an almost impossible task.

At least, George presumed Liza was dead, killed by poachers – even in that place he had chosen for its remoteness. If she were alive, she would never have abandoned her cubs. If she had been killed or crippled in a fight with some other animal, then in the area she used at that time, a circle not too far from the cubs, they would have found some remains of bones or hide in experienced and thorough searching.

Christian too had disappeared. It was possible he had changed his territory, but George thought this very unlikely.

WHAT LANDS ARE THESE?

Must all African stories end in death? Well, so did the first Christmas story. Or seemed to.

Footnote: Joy Adamson was murdered on 3rd January, 1980, near her camp in Shaba Game Reserve where she was studying leopards. Her Christmas card to us was still on the mantelpiece – a photo of Penny the leopardess, with her two minute cubs, three days old. Inside the card Joy had written 'Penny's research is fascinating, though strenuous, she is a real challenge!' Penny is the subject of her last book, published posthumously.

Seven Camps
to Rudolf

Camp 1. Samburu

WE SET OUT on our safari from Joy Adamson's house on Lake Naivasha. As Jonny Baxendale turned his blue Range Rover in at the gate, coming to pick us up, a strange lady stopped him and held out a big box of peaches.

'You're taking the Hammond Inneses on safari, aren't you? These are for your journey. They're graded for ripeness – start eating from the front and work back, they'll ripen as you go. And here's some asparagus for your first dinner in camp. They've all been picked this morning.'

Later, we were to meet this charming neighbour of Joy's (the next house along the shore of the lake) and could thank her for this delicious send-off.

Jonny Baxendale was an adventurous young man who had already done a variety of interesting things, including free-fall parachute jumping. At this time he was running safaris for people who wanted to travel on their own, pursuing their own interests and making their own timing. He had worked for two years with George Adamson, so was very close to the animals. Also, we were to discover, very easy with Africans of different tribes – relaxed, friendly, never hurried but always positive. Tall, solid, blond, experienced, a reassuring person to go into the bush with.

Ralph had worked out our route with him before we left Nairobi; we were going through the great Rift country to Mount Kulal and Lake Rudolf (now renamed Lake Turkana).

This huge lake, lying like a pendant between Kenya and Abyssinia, has always been a place of myth and legend. Discovered, as far as white people go, by Count Teleki in 1888, it was named by him after his prince, Rudolf of the hunting lodge at Mayerling. The next overland journey was made by Jonny's father and George Adamson in 1934, and in 1954 George and Joy Adamson made a very intrepid journey to South Island in a small boat, were trapped there by a change of weather, and survived in great danger, discomfort and total loneliness.

Rudolf 'the jade green sea' and its approaches seemed to exercise a powerful fascination on Ralph. In every country we visit, there is always one area which draws him like a magnet and to which our exploration of other parts of the country is a preparation, a setting of perspective. In Kenya, the potent area was irresistibly Mount Kulal and Rudolf.

Joy waved us off from her lovely house beside shining calm Naivasha. The previous evening we had sat on the closed verandah as it was quite cool, watching a family of otters come up from the lake to take food she had put out for them on the lawn. One at a time, in order of daring, they slipped and darted from cover to cover, and when there were no more plants to pause behind, they made the same crouching, hiding movement behind tufts of grass. Sinuous dark bodies, looking very small, a ballet of black shadows. And the previous afternoon we had sat out on the lawn in the sunshine watching two adult Colobus monkeys teaching a young one to jump. Their glorious long black and white fur streamed in the trees as they gradually lengthened the gap between them, so the baby leapt always to friendly arms. When he had gained confidence in jumping at the same level, one big one took up a position higher in the tree, so he could practise jumping up or down. Joy thought the two adults were mother and elder sister. They shouldn't have been there at all, but they are so persecuted for their lovely fur, that they had been driven down from the high places which were their natural home and were taking sanctuary where they could.

Here we climbed up for the first time into the blue Range Rover which was to be our new daytime home. I felt uncounted riches and marvels stretched before me, not even clearly anticipated. I knew we were going north towards the Equator, which we should cross. We should skirt Mount Kenya and drive on into the heart of Africa, that corner where Abyssinia, Uganda and Kenya meet on the shores of Lake Rudolf.

Mountains, forests, deserts . . . how strangely one adapts to a dream, and worries about little things; the ribbon tying my hat on leaving a white bar down the side of my face; the heat sitting in front and the dust sitting at the back; the carefully stacked suitcases behind me slipping on bends so I had to reach back and shove them into position – tomorrow we would tie them. Tomorrow! this would go on and on, magic unrolling day after day. The crimson of the desert rose blazing on its thorny bush, the endless pattern of the umbrella-shaped acacia tree which is the signature of East Africa. Every dead tree or shrub was used as a look-out post by some exotic bird. We saw the Pygmy Falcon, a tough, compact little bird with the predator's beak – he's very rare, I believe. We saw the Greater Bustard, all puffed up with his tail like a doll riding on his back. Saw the Secretary Bird. Ralph looked them all up in John Williams's book.*

A Field Guide to the Birds of East and Central Africa (Collins, London)

(Later, when we met him, and he took us from Nairobi to see the mating dance of the massed flamingoes by Lake Nakuru, he said no copy of his book on the birds of Kenya had ever been so well-thumbed and annotated, each unusual bird being recorded, with the place where we had seen it.) We stopped endlessly for birds, but I could not make them stop for flowers.

With Mount Kenya still mistily dominating to the east, but dropping behind us, we stopped at Nanyuki, the last town – everybody's last town going north, with very much the air of a frontier. One long wide dusty street containing everything. We stopped outside The Settlers Stores for some last minute purchases. Have we forgotten anything? They're sure to have it here, whatever it is, this is your last chance. We both bought flip-flops, and lived in them and still have them and wear them. We bought fresh fruit and some extra bottles of wine, and I wrote and posted picture postcards home, which arrived, ultimately. The serious victualling for the trip had been done by Jonny in Nairobi, and all these stores, and most of the camping equipment, were packed in our second, follow-up vehicle, a Toyota. We joined up with it here, and met the three Africans who completed our party. Peter, the driver of the Toyota, Mutungi, the cook, and Mulle, a boy to help put the camp up and down, do the daily washing, bring the food from fire to table, and be generally useful. They had all been on safari with Jonny before, but they were men from near Nairobi and had never been in the country we were going to, so it was as much an adventure to them as to us, and we were all bubbling with excitement; except Peter, who wasn't a bubbly person, a quiet man with a very nice smile. He was older than the other two, very responsible, concerned with driving and maintaining his vehicle, not dropping too far behind and getting lost, yet keeping well clear of our dust.

We stopped at two villages that day, to ensure being topped up with petrol. These were people of the Samburu tribe, with shiny, very dark skins, wearing masses of tiny bright beads; great liquid eyes and the strange pink palms of the groping hands of endless, endless, endless children – sleek and bonny; so different from the pitiful children hanging round their mothers' skirts in the mountain villages of South America. But so many of them! Could Africa hold the next generation?

Sitting in the Range Rover I was almost frightened by the sheer pressure of people round me. I didn't like to pull the doors shut, it would have seemed so unfriendly, and they were perfectly friendly and gentle. Only the numbers and the persistence and a surge of potential energy gave me a sense of discomfort, as though I might be submerged. Jonny and Ralph had wandered off. There were a few men in the crowd gathered round the car, some very old, but they were chiefly women and children. They swarmed over and into the Range Rover, repeating over and over one or two Mission school phrases in a continuous refrain, but always with a rising inflection, as though demanding an answer. (Why is 'goodbye' always the easiest phrase to learn? From Cyprus to Kenya 'Goodbye, goodbye' is called all around you as soon as you arrive. It's an easier word to say than the indeterminate 'Hullo' and serves as a general greeting, but it has a sad and final sound until you realise this.) The African 'mama' as a title of respect to any woman also takes a little getting used to. I was almost relieved when we took to the road again.

I hadn't even wondered what our camp would be like. Each moment was enough, I didn't look ahead. I always seem to arrive quite blankly at any new experience – perhaps that is why I enjoy it so much. All is as strange as magic, and as matter-of-fact as marvels in a dream.

We made camp for the first time in a clearing among big trees. The tents were all dark green canvas which did not insult the colours of the bush but blended in. They were very strong, erected on a network of metal rods slotted into each other. Ours was surprisingly roomy; a groundsheet joined the sides, so no insects could creep in; high enough to walk without thinking; a separate compartment for washing at the far end, in a collapsible canvas basin on wooden legs; two camp beds, each with a table at the foot, and a chair. The windows were of nylon mesh, you could zip solid canvas over them if you wished, but the mesh kept out mosquitoes yet allowed air and good vision. The other big tent was called the mess tent, as the table for meals was always set in its entrance. All the stores were kept inside, and Jonny slept in part of it. The three Africans preferred to sleep in the Toyota. Two slim little tents, like sentry boxes, were set a little way off and were the shower and the loo.

Jonny and Ralph and I always helped erect and break camp, and unpack and re-pack the Range Rover and the Toyota, and we soon slipped into a routine of what each person did. This first night all was set up just before dusk. Mutungi had got a fire going, and Mulle hung a canvas bucket of steaming hot water in the tree the shower was placed by. Delicious to feel the water pouring over me, and to look up through the acacia branches to the first stars! Then change into a cotton tent dress I'd bought in the heat of faraway Australia, and walk across the grass to the table set for dinner in front of the mess tent, where Jonny and Ralph had already got a bottle of red wine open. We sat over it watching Mutungi busy about his fire. Darkness stole the bush from us and we became a little bright island under the hurricane lamp hung above us on the tent, with Mutungi on a different island in the fire's glow. Then Mulle brought the first dishes; the morning's gift of asparagus, and delicious hot bread, the round flat loaves that Mutungi baked every day; then duck which we'd brought with us; cheese and fresh fruit. We were in Samburu, which is a reserve, and a tiny point of light through the trees meant another camp. This seemed wrong, but tomorrow we would be away and beyond any other visitors.

It was very peaceful going to bed in this busy, age-old world that was so complete without us. I did not feel an intruder, we were not threatening or disturbing the creatures whose home this was, we had marked out our little patch of territory like the others.

I discovered the special joy of lying in my bed looking out through the window beside me at the camp at night. The red glow of the two fires, one at each end of the camp – Mulle made them up before he went to bed. If you woke up, you could tell how far the night had advanced by whether the fires were still blazing, or had died down to a red glow. Two lanterns hung in trees – these four points of light guarded our nomadic home. I could dimly make out the square bulk of the Range Rover, the corner of the mess tent, the Toyota where the Africans slept, the flat trodden grass in the centre of the camp, and the mystery of the dark surrounding trees. I tried to stay awake, longing to see some nocturnal visitor venture cautiously into camp, or just to listen to the unknown sounds, wondering who they were and what they were doing, but always I fell asleep.

Mulle called us from deep sleep in total darkness with mugs of strong, very hot tea and a few minutes later a bucket of hot water. I woke to the sweet whistle of the mourning dove and the double note of the water-bottle bird. I washed my face in the canvas basin in front of our tent and dressed quickly in the khaki cotton shorts and top Joy Adamson had lent me – two sets – as they stand up to daily washing. We must hurry, for we were off on a 'game run' to see what we could see at a time of great animal activity, getting their breakfasts. Full light came as quickly in the morning as it faded at night, and with the rising of the sun, peace and inertia would settle upon the bush.

It was deliciously cool setting out in the thinning dark. Often we would drive and drive, slowly wandering along the tracks, and see nothing much at first; the great nests of the weaver birds, the ubiquitous blue glitter of the starlings, a great Kori Bustard. Then, suddenly, we found elephants. Quite a lot of them, moving in the short palm scrub along by the river. They were rather small – perhaps poor food in this savannah country – brown, with many young. Difficult to see in the thick low Doum palm.

'We'll go to Archer's Post, there are generally some Moran there,' Jonny said. Moran are the Samburu warriors, young men of the tribe, its traditional protectors, superbly lithe and gleaming, with red ochre on their closely and elaborately dressed hair, cloaks swung from their shoulders, all carrying spears. Now, they have little to do but be beautiful and admired. In the past, they defended the tribe in the continuous skirmishes with neighbouring tribes, hunted, and then, when only a little older, made way for their younger brothers and became 'elders' – lawmakers, the wise men, and sat under the acacia trees endlessly talking. Tribal life, though always occupied, seems to have kept a slow and measured tempo. Plenty of time just to live, before we put them into cheap western suits with cardboard suitcases under their arms, scurrying into offices, and carrying, as soon as they could afford it, that honourable insignia of civilisation, an umbrella.

The sun was already high before we returned to camp, ravenous for a hot breakfast; coffee, new bread, eggs, sausages, tinned bacon.

Here we were still within reach of tourism; we drove out during the day – soon it would be too hot for that – and visited a game dodge, beautifully situated beside a river, and had a drink in the bar. Very pleasant; but already the sight of a lot of white people, clothed, slung about with cameras and binoculars, sitting at little tables, seemed strange and somehow frightening. One wanted to escape back to camp; into cover.

Camp 2. South Horr

We left Samburu early (tea and fruit in the dark, then the tents reduced to neat piles and stowed in the Toyota, and all the small things packed in their own crates and boxes and distributed between the two vehicles with startling speed). We had decided to make a long haul to the north and approach the Rudolf area in one hard day's driving. We left just a patch of trodden grass that would soon rise, even the places where the two fires had been were raked over and already barely showed.

Passing through Archer's Post we heard a new road was open to a place with the lovely name of Maralal, so we left the main route north and slanted to the west. I looked at the map to see where we were going, and there seemed nothing there; so few lines on the page; so few names. Through Wamba to Maralal and then, far away, Baragoi. Then, a long way further north, the name South Horr. This was our objective, if possible, for the next camp. Apart from those four names, nothing.

Near Maralal we found the Toyota was no longer in sight. Had Peter merely taken a wrong track, in which case he'd soon discover this, retrace his route and follow us, or was he in any trouble? Ralph stayed at the crossroads for him, Jonny and I went on to Samburu market where, rather surprisingly, there was petrol. We wanted to fuel the vehicles and fill all the jerricans, as there'd be no chance of petrol for about a week. Peter turned up half an hour later, with Ralph on board, having had a puncture. It was market day and our cars seemed lost in a sea of tribesmen. Black, shiny, noisy, brilliant, with masses of tiny beads.

We drove then through cedar forests which were burned and blackened, their dead branches festooned with great swags of grey lichen, hanging like curtains. We stopped for a quick lunch – bread and salami and cheese and fruit and lemonade – standing on a hillside looking down over the Rift Valley. Sand devils rose and swirled down there in the hazy heat of the laval flats.

We drove a winding pass between volcanic ranges, across a dark red stony desert; the savage hard country of the Rift. Crossing a *lugga*, we turned aside from our sandy track to pause in a clearing among acacia trees. The stumps where the old branches had been broken off were polished smooth by elephants rubbing against them.

We set up camp at South Horr in under two hours, everyone working. Here we were really on our own; this was no reserve, no park, just Africa. We went for a walk as it was still light, and for the first and last time I saw Jonny with a gun, carrying it horizontally across his shoulders. The idea that this might be necessary alarmed me, but if it were to become necessary, it was reassuring that he had it. I should never have thought of being nervous otherwise, so calm is the atmosphere of the bush, the many lives weaving among each other so sensible and well-ordered. We walked through fairly thick brush, and climbing a little hill looked down at the jagged pinnacles of mountains. We found the remains of a *manyatta* where the Moran had killed cattle, probably during the solitary period of their novitiate into manhood. We were north of the Samburu tribe now, and among the Rendilli, who built very similar *manyattas*; round huts like giant beehives, thatched with small branches on a frame of light wood (or if they can get it, chicken-wire).

This was rhino country, full of the sweet-smelling bush they like to feed on, and the strong tangy scent in the air was the smell of black rhino. The moist ground down by the *lugga* was criss-crossed with rhino and buffalo tracks, but we saw nothing.

Towards the end of our safari, when we'd all got to know each other well, I asked Jonny why he'd taken a gun that time, that time only. Was it to impress us at the outset that the bush was real, so we didn't behave stupidly and treat it as though it were the English countryside? No, he would not admit that. He gave the perfectly sensible reason that where we had been walking was thickly wooded, and if you did come upon anything, it would be very sudden and very close – which generally speaking is the only danger.

At South Horr, acacia trees were again our walls, our roof-tree. Suddenly there seemed far more stars. The smell of the tooth-brush bush filled the camp – the tribesmen use twigs of it to whiten their teeth.

By day, little groups of Rendilli women came and squatted just beyond our camp, silently watching us, just watching; only their eyes moved. So quiet and still they were, it was surprising to forget them, look again, and find them still there. Jonny went and talked to them. I didn't notice that our Africans did. They had little in common with these Northern tribes, and were afraid of things being stolen.

Already we five were growing into a very close little community. Although Peter and Mutungi and Mulle were doing this as a job, it was a job they had chosen because they enjoyed it, and wanted a chance to see a different part of Kenya – they were all from near Nairobi. Peter, a Kikuyu, was actually from the town, chiefly interested in cars and very good with them.

He'd been to Mission school, and spoke some English, so we could talk to him. Mutungi and Mulle were of the Wa-Kamba, and were countrymen, so were more reserved, also less used to white people. Speaking no English, we could only talk to them through Jonny. But when we happened to meet Mutungi in Jonny's office in Nairobi long afterwards, he wrung our hands with beaming smiles as old friends who had shared an adventure. Their obvious enjoyment and interest in all the new discoveries was a part of our days.

The Rendilli are a camel people. Here, for the first time, driving out from South Horr camp, we saw herds of camels and herds of donkeys. The young women are superbly beautiful in their gleaming black nakedness, with the massed bead necklaces, and an arrogant backward-arched carriage. They carry a cloth slung from one shoulder to another cloth slung from the hip to carry a baby, or a black gourd for water. They stand with perfect poise beside the road to watch us go by. Under the shade of the central tree in the villages, the elders sit in a circle on the hard dusty ground talking and gesticulating – but they are not old at all! In the red glow of their ochre the Moran in their prime elaborately adorn and dress each other's hair. It is not advisable to photograph them, unless you are very skilful with a telescopic lens and cunning at concealing it. They know what cameras do, and are against a representation of themselves being in your possession to take away. It might give you some sort of power over them. Every village is running with bouncy black children of every size. What will become of them? There are too many now for any land to support.

The long necks of giraffes sprout from the acacia trees. The huge round bulk of ostriches on tiny legs looks so artificial, from the distance like black boulders on the dusty plain. The zebras here are the beautiful Grévy's, the zebra of the north. Their stripes are brown, instead of black, and differently patterned, and the animals are larger. The infinite variety of the gazelle family, from the dainty little 'Thomies', up through the larger Grants – these two always in fairly large groups, with their distinctively different marking, but the same dainty fleetness of movement, the same hair-spring alertness of creatures whose only safety is in their speed, the same smooth and silky coats, the gentle heads and great eyes. Always they graze in close groups for protection. Brown kites hang in the sky, and still there are brilliant red outbreaks of the desert rose. Once we surprised a great Bateleur eagle, not nailed to the sky like a crucifix, but perched on a dead tree, so we could actually see his red beak and legs.

I always came upon our camp with surprise, so well the group of dark green tents blended into the bush. Suddenly we would be home, to Mulle washing yesterday's clothes in a great pan of steaming water, then pegging them out on a line, and at the other side, Mutungi stooping over the white ashes baking the bread. Or to the warning shadow of darkness, stars, the heavenly shower under the acacia, the lanterns in the trees, the fires, a drink in the glorious cool outside the mess tent, Mutungi supervising his cooking pots, then Mulle coming over with the dishes. Then each day's final magic, going to bed beside the mesh window and watching the camp at night; listening, trying to keep awake; but always falling into sleep, sleep. How long had this life gone on? Must it ever end – was there any other way of living?

This safari, as so much of our sailing had done, merged into a pattern. The rhythm of game-runs morning and evening, always unpredictable, the alert watching, the surprise and excitement of each discovery; the infinite peace of the camp, so complete and self-contained, surrounded and protected by the strong and busy bush. The world we had left retreated further and further in time and place, remembered, if at all, as something hysterical and dangerously manufactured.

We stayed several nights at each camp site, so that driving out and back we found the same individual animals always in the same place, the same birds on the expected tree; we had become part of a settled and familiar community. Breaking camp and setting it up, packing and unpacking the Range Rover and the Toyota, the same things always in the same place; all this produced a dreamlike sense that this way of life was the only one, had always been like this; would go on for ever.

The last night at South Horr was also the last night of the old year, 31 December. I remembered my home, my village, my friends. Was that other world still there?

Camp 3. In the Doum Palms by Lake Rudolf

Choking sand, intolerable heat, and a dangerously violent wind are my memories of our camp in a stretch of Doum palms a little way above the lake edge. We had come into a harsh and barren land.

At the beginning of the day, driving out of the north end of the South Horr valley, it was still the Africa we had come to know and expect; family groups of the great reticulated giraffe, dreamlike in their fluid, slow-motion beauty of movement; a rare gerenuk, the big gazelle with the long neck who feeds on the leaves of trees – indeed, standing on his hind legs with his front legs dangling and his head lifted to eat above him, he appears to be hanging from the tree; Rendilli tribesmen with their herds of camels and goats. But the bush began to thin, the acacia trees became few and far between and very small. The heat became more intense than any we had known, it was a dark red stony world. There was no life but a few ground birds. A high wind from behind us made the dust a real problem. The mass of Kulal ahead loomed bigger and bigger. The sky was a hard incredible blue over the still unseen lake. The track worsened, we were driving through a waste of lava, boulders of it piled beside the road, and volcanic vents.

There was a Mission at Loiyangalani beside the lake, and to get their Bedford trucks through they had laid concrete ramps over the worst patches of road, which stopped so abruptly that we had to get down and pile stones under the Range Rover's wheels to prevent damage to our sump, Jonny easing her gently down from each, Peter in the heavily laden Toyota following at a careful snail's pace. Each time we got out, the sun's heat hit like a blow.

We climbed through the volcanic outcrops to the edge of the lava escarpment, and there below us, at last, lay Rudolf – blue! very blue, not the legendary green at all, and flecked with whitecaps like the sea. South Island was a dark lump of volcanic rock. We were looking at the southern end of the lake, which extends north for 180 miles, and ends between Ethiopia and the Sudanese border.

The only possible camp site was in the oasis of Doum palms running along a ridge. It had taken half an hour to creep down from the escarpment and was now full noonday heat. We decided to put up only minimum tents, and to lash them to the stoutest palm trees for security, else they would have blown away. This was oven heat, and the harsh sand-laden wind scratched and choked us. For the first time, I hadn't enough energy to make my (very small) contribution to putting up camp. They unpacked the little canvas chair from our tent and put it in the deepest shade. There I sat, looking, Ralph said, like the classic white lady of olden times, sitting on a chair in the middle of nowhere watching the slaves work.

Peter, who insisted on helping unpack the Toyota though he had had a gruelling morning's driving, began to have that curious bloomy-grey look of a black-skinned person who is not well. He was sweating profusely, and admitted he had a headache. Jonny made him sit down in the least hot place. Malaria was the unspoken fear in everyone's mind. What would this mean? Driving to the Mission to radio for the Flying Doctor Service to fetch him to hospital. For us, it would mean Ralph taking over the driving of the second vehicle, and the energy and concentration this would need, would greatly reduce the value of the expedition, as the whole point was for him to see, think, notice and remember as much as possible. But we were chiefly concerned for Peter, it was very distressing to see him looking like this, he was such a nice person in his quiet, serious, slightly worried way.

'There's just one other possibility,' Jonny said. 'Salt deficiency. I've given him some salt tablets. We'll see if they have any effect.' Within a surprisingly short time, Peter bobbed up, not perspiring any more, colour natural, headache gone, smiling his nice smile, himself again.

But enough was wrong at Rudolf. We visited the Mission, where a rather cross missionary was pouring out instructions to his Africans about some celebration that night. The El Molo, traditional fishermen of this southern shore of Rudolf, being discouraged from the nomadic habits of their tribe, and encouraged to build more and more permanent *manyattas*, are destroying the oasis. Clinging on to the assistance of the Mission, their numbers increase steadily and fast, their natural skills are forgotten, being no longer essential to life, and the energy and self-reliance of their character deteriorates. I had been shocked, since coming to East Africa, by the inference of despairing criticism with which missionaries were spoken of. From now on, I began to see why. It is not easy to draw a line between feeding the hungry and healing the sick; and then proceeding to establish conditions which cause the population to increase so that the country is gradually devoured.

My mother, a step-child feeling herself unwanted at home, had run away to India to be a missionary – a blend of adventure and idealism characteristic of her. Being a missionary then meant casting out fear and horror, and replacing them with hope and faith. That seems a lost dream. Little radiance, little that is spiritual at all, seems to linger in these purely material organisers of unnatural ways of life. Small nomadic tribes of great character, their numbers controlled by seasonal food supplies, are replaced by a dependent people encouraged to spread and spread. The African governments also discourage tribes from being nomadic, as they are difficult to control. But *manyattas*, mealy patches and cattle give the land no chance to renew itself.

Ralph was determined to get a good look at South Island if possible. A business enterprise had been started recently to offer fishing on Lake Rudolf. Boats had been trucked up, and fishermen could fly in from Nairobi. The attraction was tilapia, the Nile perch which can run up to 200 lbs on Rudolf. The Mission had a curious monster of a slab-sided boat in a corrugated iron shed with a concrete slipway; her plates had been trucked up and welded on the spot. The Mission were also building a fish plant, an industry to employ the now idle and unoccupied El Molo and their teeming children ... and to finish the tilapia.

We haunted the gritty, smelly and eye-searing beach, trying to persuade the owner of the fishing boats to take us round South Island. He was understandably reluctant, as the wind had been blowing 70 knots during the night and was still high. Four Italians had just arrived at the airstrip for a few hours' fishing. However, they were finally sent off in the smaller boat with all their elaborate tackle, and the owner agreed to circumnavigate the island with us in his larger boat, which he drove himself – unless the wind rose.

After a few jittery hours of trying to assess wind force on the different sides of the island, we set off in the early afternoon. The glare from the water screwed one's eyes to slits. Everything was gritty. The sweaty owner passed us sticky bottles of tepid Coke.

I tried to think about the wild history of this island; the expedition lost there, never accounted for; the Adamsons' desperate sojourn there. The many mysteries; for instance, how did the goats get there? I tried to concentrate on the place itself, in the north the bare lava coloured red to black; monstrously big crocodiles slid off the rocks at our approach. I remembered that on another part of the lake, a French leather company had been granted a concession to kill crocodiles for a short period, and had put their short time to such savage use that they had practically eliminated them in that area.

On the west side there are gentler slopes, some grass, even a few stunted acacia trees, the mysterious goats grazing. The south and east are again wild laval slopes. The boat cut the waves at speed, the wind had dropped.

I have never failed to respond to any place as completely as to South Island, or, indeed, to Lake Rudolf on this first visit. Later, we were to come again to the Jade Green Sea.

But I have one lovely memory of our camp in the Doum palms! The last evening we drove north along the shore, to walk through sandhills to the shining edge of the water, and watch in glimmering sunset light a multitude of water birds and waders – flamingo, toucan, pelicans, and a myriad smaller ones. The burial hills grew blacker, storks came flapping in, and the sand seemed moving with doves.

At night the wind blew again, very strongly, and I fell asleep hoping the ropes would hold that lashed our tent to the palm trees. But sometimes the palms were uprooted themselves.

The only camp I was not sorry to pack up and leave.

Camp 4. Kulal

Kampi ya Mawingo we called our camp near the top of Kulal; 'Camp in the Clouds'.

Kulal is a great mass of mountain, split into ranges and gorges by the prehistoric cataclysm which formed the Rift. I did not know what character of mountain it was, nor how high up we could go.

We left Lake Rudolf by a very new road, so new that we met the last of the road gangs who had worked on it just leaving; the tracks of their Bedford the only tracks on the road, and saw the signpost Loiyangalani set up where the new road joined the old.

We left our old South Horr track and turned up towards Kulal, the heat gradually going out of the wind as we climbed, and the country softening to grass and occasional trees. I remember a female ostrich with her five young, their pale brown feathers fluttering in the breeze – no wonder they are called 'strawbacks' – and a superb group of three male ostriches. We saw herds of Oryx, always so elegant and well-groomed with their sleek pale coats and decorative twisted horns; groups of the big sepia-striped Grévy's zebra, giraffes, with their bodies under a tree but their periscope heads always lifted and vigilant. We skimmed the edge of a long valley, climbing sharply, then came upon many tribesmen with cattle.

We stopped at the only building we were to see on this journey, the Mission house. This very special missionary (to our great disappointment he was away on leave) was a man of vision who truly loved and respected Africa. Determined that his Africans should not drive their herds into the indigenous forest above the Mission and destroy it, he had taught and encouraged them to dig by hand a trench 120 feet deep to bring down water from the mountain – a most ambitious, most efficient piece of irrigation, running for roughly four or five miles. Two men of the missionary's household came out to greet us and explain his absence, also his two dogs, a long-haired Alsatian and an Airedale.

From then on the track was narrow and very rough, through high primeval forest. We crawled up slowly, followed by the Toyota. One can seldom say that one's vehicles are the first any-where, but very few people have gone on to climb above the Mission – I do not know of any. From time to time we had to get out to move trees that had been pushed across the tracks by elephants, either by pulling at the branches or rubbing them-selves. The path grew wetter, so that we had to get cut branches to throw down in front of the vehicles to give a surface over mud patches; sometimes we had to lop trees just to clear enough room to pass. Branches swept the Range Rover on both sides, it was dangerous to leave an elbow sticking out. The thick cover of trees made it dark. The high forest that soared up to the light we could not see, was choked with giant creepers; every tree had other, smaller trees growing from it, and these secondary trees had enormous ferns growing from them. It was now – incredibly! – a rain forest, with the teeming, almost personal sense of movement this wild proliferation in the moisture creates. Occasional trees of frightening size, age and character stood out like chieftains of the forest. The lush green of a rain forest seems to have a rather malignant life in every tendril. You feel they would hit you, or entwine you, if you got in their way.

We realised the Airedale had followed us all the way, rather to our concern. The Alsatian had soon been pulled back by his conscience, knowing it was his responsibility to guard the house in his master's absence.

Very near the top of Kulal, we found a little open glade on the slope of a hill, with a spring of water. Here we set up camp. There was a chill little wind, and everything was damp. While we were putting up the tents the two Africans from the Mission arrived, having followed us in their Land Rover. They had come to retrieve the Airedale (a sparkling, amiable dog) but also, we felt, as an adventure. They had never been up here before, and took the opportunity of following the track we had opened. They warned us about the Wandrobo, a secretive forest people seldom seen, of whom the tribesmen are very wary. They say the Wandrobo are so swift and silent they can take anything left about a camp without being seen; they are generally harmless.

Mutungi ran down the slope to fetch water from the spring, while Mulle searched for sticks dry enough to start a fire. We sat close to it to eat our dinner, wearing everything we had, warming our hands on the hot soup mugs. We were in a little sloping green room whose walls were trees of which we could not see the top. I had dragged a Husky through this safari, and on top of Kulal I was glad to have it as an eiderdown on my bed, as well as wearing it during the day.

From Kampi ya Mawingo we walked on higher, butterflies as big as birds flickering in the trees, and always the strange sense a rain forest gives of being in a state of movement, alive in a more restless, aggressive way than other woods . . . The track was stony; we climbed steeply, then crossed a little ravine, and climbed through a coppice. I was out of breath, also fascinated by a profusion of small flowers, all new to me. The most frequent was a tawny-yellow plumbago which grew everywhere, quite close to the ground, not a climber. I started to pick a few flowers of each variety, arranging them in my hand so that each kind showed individually. I would ask Ralph to photograph them, so I would have a colour print to show our gardener.

I realised Jonny and Ralph had gone a long way, and I was afraid of being lost, so raced up after them through the trees and came out on to a grassy open hillside. There was a belt of bush below me to the right, and just above it, sitting on the grass with their backs to me, chatting among themselves, were some of the largest baboons I had ever seen. These baboons on top of Kulal are giants. They were just sitting about, moving from time to time to speak to each other; I presume they saw me, but they paid no attention. Except that they one by one dropped down into the cover of the bush. If they had come towards me I should have yelled with terror, however harmless their curiosity might have been. I had often watched the agility and strength of ordinary baboons, but these hairy old men of the mountain were enormous.

I came upon Ralph and Jonny sitting on what looked like the bunker of a golf course, a ridgy outcrop that gave some protection from the wind. And there below, miles below, lay Rudolf.

We came repeatedly to this look-out post. Once we found two Africans with spears sitting there – not Wandrobo as I had secretly hoped, wanting to see some, but two Samburu who grazed their cattle on a pinnacle of grass in the centre of the gorge below, and were looking for a way to get them across to new grazing. (How had they ever got them there, I wondered?) It was very cold, but they wore only a blanket round them, and on a necklace of small beads a little wooden box containing tobacco – for chewing, not smoking though they seemed to enjoy the cigarettes Ralph offered them. Jonny was very good at talking to people – not just the language, but his whole approach.

Sometimes from this high green knoll mist streamed along the gorge below, hiding the great lake, suddenly revealing South Island through a rent, then closing again. The torrential downpours fortunately happened when we were in camp. Bursts of sunshine came in the late afternoon bringing out the butter-flies; many yellow swallow-tails, dazzling little sunbirds, par-rots, turacos green as the leaves that concealed them, peering down at us with interest. Droppings of the Greater Kudu were everywhere, but we never saw that shy and lovely gazelle. Cloud poured in before the sunset. Watching from the edge of the forest we saw it burn up and disappear in the heat rising from Rudolf. This vortex was where the violent 70 knot wind was engendered that swept the southern shore of the lake.

But where we were, the cloud surrounded us, isolating us on the tiny island of wet and vivid ground, immediately around us, very alone with storm and mountain. The nights were clear, the stars brilliant, both the true and the false Southern Cross hanging over the forest. And it was very cold.

Camp 5. Desert Camp, Kargi

Ralph was very anxious I should have the experience of camping in the desert. He had spent some time in the North African desert during the war, and like so many Englishmen, especially, perhaps, those who are drawn to the sea, had been fascinated by it. There is the same sense of limitless space and freedom, discovery and cleanness. So we planned to break the journey to Marsabit, the great forest reserve of the North, by spending one night at Kargi, the south-western end of the vast Chalbi desert.

When we left Kulal, driving down the forest track through an area of particularly high trees, we stopped to consider one of gigantic stature and curious formation. Its wood was very dark, and it had an exaggerated air, like an impressionist drawing of a tree of great antiquity rather than a real tree. It had a very strong personality. It was traditionally regarded as a sacred tree (to save it from being cut down, presumably). So absorbed were we in discussing it that we missed the half-concealed turning off to the Mission, and continued a long way down the mountain on a false trail that ended in a water-hole, the ground all round trampled to a morass. The rain had been heavy on this side of the mountain, and the Toyota bogged down in a steep uphill gully as we retraced our path. We were some time rebuilding the track with stones and branches before she finally made it. Ralph remarked that a less well-mounted safari would have been in real trouble, and a bigger safari, with trucks, could not have gone where we had been. It was good of Jonny to risk his beautiful new Range Rover in ascending Kulal.

Below the Mission we ran into rain, interrupted by flickers of sun, and looking down into the steaming, mist-patched gorge, we saw several dainty, vivid rainbows far below us. Later I took a photograph of Ralph drinking out of his hand, water scooped from a puddle! – something unheard of and ridiculous in the Chalbi desert, one of the earth's driest regions.

The moisture brought out all the brilliant birds on to the spare black thorn bushes, and again John Williams's book came out to identify them, and note in it where we had seen the rarer ones, for his interest when we came back. The rarest of all was a swallow-tailed kite. We also identified a black-shouldered kite and black-bellied bustards; also many shrikes – that evening-dress bird with his white shirt front and very black head and neck.

We made a tiny camp in the desert. Flat firm sand with a dark pattern of low thorn bushes here and there.

We put up just the top of the big mess tent, no sides or ground sheet, and in it three beds for Jonny and Ralph and me. Peter and Mutungi and Mulle slept as usual in the Toyota. No shower or loo. Mutungi made a quick little fire from dry thorn, and gave us hot water, then supper.

The stars were multitudinous, as there was nothing to block

out the sky, which stretched without limit. They seemed stiller than usual; painted, not sparkling.

I cannot explain the feeling this place gave me. I had seen deserts before – the north of the Sahara, the edge of the Gibson in West Australia, the Sechura in Peru; but I had not been a part of them in the sense of going to sleep and waking up, an unknown distance from any other people, buildings or vehicles. I had not belonged to them.

Curiously, it was not dead but very much alive, a personality all its own, as I don't remember any birds or animals, and there was no sound. But wandering off in the early morning a little way from camp, I found tiny heaps of small bones in some places, neatly assembled where they had stopped living, and I felt that I too could lie down and leave my bones among the others, peacefully and without sorrow. It was not of the world but outside the world, and outside time. I have never had anything remotely resembling this feeling anywhere else. I shall never forget it.

Camp 6. *Paradise Lake, Marsabit*

At Marsabit we camped beside Paradise Lake. To reach it, we drove a very long narrow track through forest, which I found a little frightening; the bush was high and thick and close on either side. I always remember it as I saw it first, with a buffalo standing in the middle of the track, looking at us. I had heard the black buffalo described as the most formidable animal in Africa. The extraordinary level spread of thick horns meeting to armour-plate the heavy head, and the solid bulk of the body, suggest terrifying momentum. The way they lower their heads to look at you gives a sullen, truculent expression, and when they lift their heads to scent you, they tilt them slightly, which gives a (quite erroneous) impression of calling up reinforcements. In fact, I think they are just short-sighted, and are trying to find out what you are, also why; when they finally turn away, they always stop and turn round to give you a second look. They are gregarious when young, but old bulls get pushed out of the herd to live alone, or in little groups of similar outcasts. Their lowered heads are defence against even a rhino, and an elephant will turn aside from a herd bull. One lion will not attack a buffalo alone, it needs two.

Jonny drove on slowly, and he wandered off, as they generally do – he was only curious.

We drove this approach track every day, to and from our various expeditions. I remember frequent elephant noises in the bush, once very close and persistent on my side. I think they were parallelling us for a little way, hidden in the thick greenery.

Our camp site was glorious; on level ground between the lake and a wall of rocks. There was a colony of baboons in these rocks, quite small ones compared to the great Men of Kulal. Sometimes at night they kept up a great hubbub. There must have been a leopard – their great enemy – on the prowl. Every evening two elephants came down to drink on the opposite side of the lake, the same two, moving the same distance round the edge of the water in such extraordinary slow motion that each would stand for a perceptible pause with one foot lifted before putting it on the ground. Sitting outside, watching them over a drink, I used to wonder idly what would happen if they ever continued their evening stroll round the lake far enough to reach us. There was something implacable, quite unstoppable, about this slow advance. Would they just proceed through the camp, picking their way carefully between our tents? Probably, like most animals, they would avoid intruding upon others.

Mutungi and Mulle wanted to make an expedition one morning, I think to a village celebration they had heard about. They proposed walking to the road, and hoping some vehicle of the Reserve's transport would come along and give them a lift. Jonny offered them the Toyota, but they said they preferred to walk. I thought it very intrepid of them, remembering that narrow track – about three miles – through dense forest. True, they were both countrymen (Peter didn't want to go) but they were from a very different part of Kenya; also they were going in the middle of the day, when the animals are usually resting and don't want to be bothered. However, I was very relieved when they came safely back to camp in the late afternoon.

One evening we saw an extraordinary bird-battle over the lake. A Fish Eagle came to catch his supper, and against this danger all the small water-birds on the lake, who usually kept in strict groups according to kind, ignoring each other or occasionally having brief skirmishes, ganged up to protect their home and their fish from this unfair competition. This battle went on for some time, the great invader swooping again and again above the flocks of little birds below, while they massed and screamed and fluttered in anger. He could not get through to the water, because wherever he came down there was a shifting mass of small birds rising to protect their water and drive him off. In the end he gave up and soared off to search other water – a long way away. We were glad, because if a Fish Eagle had established himself on Paradise Lake, he would have reduced the stock of fish till there was not enough to support the others.

At the other end of Marsabit – another world, it seemed – we visited the game warden's lodge, an open space with flowering trees, sleeping quarters, a cafeteria, showers. A group of tourists had just come in. They were on a shooting safari, their vehicles slung about with corpses. Their voices, clothes, faces and conversation were exactly those which have been pilloried so often, from Romain Gary's *Roots of Heaven* to Thurber's cartoons and countless others, it was difficult to believe they could still exist. But their guns were real and their animals were dead.

The game wardens' talk was of Ahmed, the elephant who had become famous because of his fabulous size. Later, Kenyatta was to take him under his personal protection – a rather ironical publicity gesture, I thought, considering the bulk of ivory being exported from Kenya from all the other elephants. We did not see Ahmed, nor did I greatly care. I thought much more about another elephant, a female who had been shot in Marsabit the previous night. She had been shot by Marsabit guards driving along the main road (which crosses the Reserve) on their way home, going off duty. They said she had suddenly appeared in the road and threatened them and they shot her in self-defence. Jonny was angrier than I had ever seen him, he called it licensed murder. He thought it very unlikely she had threatened them, they had panicked unnecessarily. She would have been dazzled by their headlights, and made the usual little mock charge towards the possible source of danger. If they'd switched off their headlights so she could see, even fired a shot over her head 'if they'd got to play guns', she would probably have gone off. They were, after all, regular employees of the Reserve, they were supposed to know something of animal behaviour.

She had travelled some way after she had been shot, trying to reach cover, and now lay on her side several hundred yards from the road. She was still in milk, so somewhere a very young elephant calf was dying, unless it was lucky enough to find another cow elephant in milk. One thought of the twenty-two-month gestation, the two years before weaning, the protection and concern of the herd at a birth and the long care afterwards, the participation of the whole group in the event, and their terrible distress when harm came to one of them; the four-year interval between calving. Now there she lay, alone, beginning to smell, the flies clotting on her.

A steady line of Africans walked from the road to look at her, so that a track was trodden to the grey mound. How had so many heard so quickly? – it drew them like a summons. I cannot define, but I cannot forget, the look on the faces of those coming back from viewing the dead elephant. This was something primeval, atavistic. Perhaps 'gratified' expresses it best, or 'fulfilled'. I had seen exactly the same look once before, on the faces of another line of strangers coming away from a viewing. That had been in New York, when I went to Central Station to see the big public TV screen showing the first landing of astronauts on the moon. Another tribe who had been handed a vicarious victory over something which had been too big for their ancestors.

From camp we used to go in the evening to a look-out which

Jonny called Hurricane Hill. From here you looked down in all directions over the country spread below. Here the elephants poured out of the forest to search for food when the tribesmen and their herds were gone, and the natural inhabitants could venture out to look for what was left. I counted twenty elephants, spreading out over the plain; then I turned and saw more in the other direction, singly and in little groups. Also giraffes in family groups. The elephants were *pink*. I thought it was a trick of the light, some sunset glow, until first one, and then another, syphoned up the red earth and blew it back over himself, turning for a moment brick-red, then, after shaking himself and walking a few steps out of the pink cloud, emerged rose-colour. They looked small and toy-like seen from above, but by comparison of size, some must have been enormous.

We saw the Greater Kudu too, in the evening foraging time, as we scrambled up some hillocks covered with coarse grass, near enough to see the thin white lines on their backs like a striped blanket, a total disguise when standing among branches – these large, rare and shy antelope, living in pairs or small family groups, not herds. And one day Jonny took us to a very secret place. We left the Range Rover and walked through the bush a little way, so as not to leave a car track which others might follow. We arrived at a water-hole regularly used by elephants. The tribesmen had not found it – anyway, it was too buried to get their herds to – so the elephants had it to them-selves to drink, and wallow in the mud-baths they love. I was nervous for fear one came and found us there. The pool was ringed in greenery. A very private place. Peace lay thick around it, something tangible. Once it had all been like this. Jonny said, 'This is what we're fighting for.'

The last terrifying day, we saw the Rendilli watering their herds. Terrifying because of the numbers. An old Cecil B. de Mille Hollywood epic would have showed only tiny, token crowds by comparison. I had never really imagined numbers 'like the sands of the sea'. The Rendilli watered their herds twice a week, and conducted it like a military operation. A man stood with one foot in a water-hole, calling the cattle – almost a continuous singing – and the herdsmen brought them down group by group for their timed turn of drinking, then drove them on, and the next herd took their place. Looking up the mountain, one saw cattle pouring down like rivers converging on the water-hole.

This was on the other side of the mountain from our camp, but had once been a part of Marsabit. It was a visually clear demonstration of how the wild country was being eaten up by the ever-increasing herds of cattle. Cattle kept to show prestige, wealth in the fact of their possession, like jewellery or pictures, very little used in any way. Literally eating out the country. Forests are cut to increase the grazing, heading towards a dust-bowl. Whereas the infinite variety of fauna who are born to occupy the African bush, eat at different levels, many are nomadic within a large area, they have maintained and regenerated Africa through the millennia.

Camp 7. Meru

And so, on our way back to Naivasha, we came at last to Meru.

I think it is true to say that Meru as a National Park would not have come into being if not for the Adamsons. Though they have had no connection with it for many years, surely this must always be remembered. Meru is where the Elsa story happened. When anything becomes so famous, when any name becomes a household word, a legend, it is difficult to realise that it was ever real. Joy Adamson said to us once, 'So much! So much! All this . . . They would like to make an industry of Elsa. Sometimes even I almost lose touch with what it really was, how it all started.'

But here, once upon a time, a lady and a lioness spent their siesta together during the long, breathless afternoons. Joy often lay with her head on Elsa's back 'because it was comfortable, the most convenient pillow I had handy', and looking back later, she told us she thought this drowsy, relaxed physical contact had much to do with their later trust in each other. From that clearing in the bush, a story reached out to excite and touch the whole world. Probably no other single animal has, by the story of her life, done so much to make people understand that animals are individual personalities, feeling, experiencing, making decisions. By her relationship with the Adamsons, continued by her own deliberate choice and conduct, she forced the world to question the ethic of zoos, seeing them as prisons for other animals who were also Born Free. That so much was known about such a highly-developed animal personality underlined the age-old atrocity of performing animals as being inadmissible.

Joy would say, 'It is not George and I who made Meru, it is Elsa. Meru is her memorial.' Her photograph has been placarded in every city in the world, she has been impersonated by other lionesses in films; but here she lived, from the dependent cub taken about on a lead to a free adult lioness, wild, mated, independent, yet bringing her cubs into camp. When she was dying, and in great agony, she came to sit beside George Adamson and from time to time lifted her head to rub against his face, as if seeking comfort.

She is buried here, but her grave is known to very few people, as Joy did not want it to become a showplace for tourists. The best-known animal who ever lived has still the privacy they fought to keep for her in life – now so desperately sought by the living animals who remain. For me Meru is always Elsa-haunted.*

It is now run by an extremely able and enterprising game warden who, when we were there, was grappling with the major problem; how to ensure that tourists saw enough animals to enjoy themselves, and so keep the place economically viable, and at the same time to avoid disturbing the animals so much they either disappeared, or became unnaturally over familiar with humans so that they lost their natural fear of people, their

*After Joy's murder in 1980, and her simple funeral in Isiola, George took her ashes to Meru and scattered them in the neighbourhood of Elsa's grave.

instinct to avoid anything strange, and became potentially dangerous.

He had planned a pattern of intersecting roads, rather like New York, with signposts at the crossroads. He wanted to restrict motor traffic to a road circling the Park, and to keep the interior roads for foot or camel 'safaris', accompanied by a game warden. When we were there, the approach roads prevented too great a number of tourists, but that would change, must change, if the place was to survive. Given the problem, it is difficult to see how anyone could plan better.

We camped by the Tana River, in a little clearing. It was quite narrow here, and on the opposite bank lived a colony of Vervet monkeys – tiny, fairy monkeys, suddenly filling a tree, chattering, pulling the leaves, swinging, then disappearing in a flash, as if blown away, to reappear a moment later in a different tree. Irresistible to watch them – where would they swoop again, how many of them, how many babies, clinging to miniature mothers?

A profusion of animals filled our early morning and our evening runs. We seemed to be driving along endless rides through an enchanted forest. As usual, we would start off by going for some time seeing nothing very much, and wonder if today we would draw a blank, and go home disappointed. ('As

usual'? 'going home'? But this must end ... Could it end, this way of life that had become so familiar?)

Then something wonderful would suddenly be there; a family of black rhinos, male, female and calf, a rare group to see, taking shape through a camouflaging tracery of leaves, seen only because they moved slowly as they grazed; another black rhino alone, in a different area. Hippos basking in the pool of a stream where it passed under a little bridge, only their snouts showing, difficult to pick out among bits of wood, or rock, or fallen leaves. Gentle plump water-buck. A beautiful sight of an Oryx, one of the grandest of all the antelopes. Hartebeeste, with the V-shaped horns. Giraffes. Large herds of buffalo; better stop to let them pass; some buffalo with their tough, stocky black calves – we hadn't seen buffalo with young before.

So many tribes of animals sharing the same place, living their separate lives without conflict, going quietly their individual ways without disturbing each other. At the evening feeding time, especially, the place was rich and alive with creatures great and small, from the immensely powerful, to the small ones who were quite defenceless except for scent and speed.

Once, cruising slowly along a ride – Ralph standing in the back with his head up through the sunshine roof – Jonny said, 'Better duck, Ralph, there's a spitting cobra beside the path. They can shoot the venom quite a long way.' I saw the dark curving line in the track. Without thought I expected Jonny to drive over it – don't people always kill snakes? – but he drove round it. Back in camp I asked him, 'Why didn't you kill the cobra? Is it because this is a Reserve, and everything has the right to live?', and he nodded.

In Meru we saw bull elephants alone, and cow elephants with calves, in their usual family groups, these matriarchs bringing up young from tiny ones walking beneath them, to half-grown adolescents of ten or fifteen years. All our old friends we saw again – ostriches, balls of fluff on stilts – as well as many new. We saw for the first time the white rhino, lumbering yellow beasts with wide mouths. As if giving us a final profusion to remember.

The last morning, as we were leaving Meru, a pair of jackals came quite slowly down a grassy ride towards us. As far as four-legged beasts can, they gave an impression of being hand-in-hand, their bearing was so affectionate and companionable. They were particularly beautiful jackals, this animal varies so much. They were long-haired, with a lot of gold about them. These two setting out so happily to start their day, so leisurely and relaxed, an almost dancing walk, will always leap to my mind unbidden when I remember that lost world. 'We must come back!' we said. But how much is there now to go back to? The pace of the slaughter has quickened so sharply, the wild areas so encroached upon in the last few desperate years.

That morning Mutungi had called us with tea for the last time, and Mulle produced hot water. When camp was broken, the personal things were separated from the equipment. We left just as it was beginning to get light, leaving the beautiful clearing to the Vervets, and to any other visitors. On the way out, we waited for the last big stampede of buffaloes across our path. Outside the Reserve, we passed again through the *shambas*, where the Meru people seemed consistently scowling and dour after the Samburu and the Rendilli – let alone the spectacular, show-off Masai whom we had seen further south.

We drove up into the Aberdare mountains. Here we saw the wild floating grace of the Colobus monkeys again. This was one of the places where they should be, the level from which the family we had watched in Joy's garden must have been driven. We were lucky to see any, they are so shy and swift in flight, and no wonder, they've learned that the coming of men usually means death or capture.

We had a hasty and rather cold picnic in light mist, with unseen elephants rumbling away in the undergrowth beside the Pass, then climbed up into the Range Rover for the last stretch of the journey back to Naivasha.

We had set out to search for a strange country, a secret and timeless place which had existed, unchanged, since long before our own kind had emerged. And we had indeed found it, watched and for a time been a part of that busy, active, well-ordered world of infinite variety. But we had seen it to be a country invaded, its natural inhabitants a population of fugitives in retreat. No longer secret, but everywhere opened up and taken over, the animals driven into smaller and smaller areas, the traps closer together, the necessary food scarcer and more dangerous to go in search of, the quiet places to breed and educate the young no longer there; the world prices of their skins and tusks always rising as their numbers dwindled.

Private fortunes are being amassed from skins, ivory and charcoal, and the souvenir shops in Nairobi found buyers for every scrap of a dead animal they could make into something to sell – even cuff-links from the tiny paws of the dik-dik – to the very tourists who had come to Africa to see the last of the game! In March 1978, a law came into force prohibiting the sale of wild animal products. Whether this will really take the ultimate threat out of poaching, or to what extent it will just deflect it to a black market and export, remains to be seen. The only real relief will be if people stop buying. So long as people want skins and ivory, so long they will be provided, somehow. Exploitation of animals seems to be the new slave trade. But here there can be no redress, because as Joseph Conrad said, 'Animals cannot make a revolution.'

> *Into my heart an air that kills*
> *From yon far country blows*
>
> *That is the land of lost content*
> *I see it shining plain.*
> *The happy highways where I went,*
> *And may not come again.*

A Strong and Secret Place

Richard Leakey's Camp at Koobi Fora

SHORTLY BEFORE we went to Africa, Richard Leakey made world headlines. He had discovered a human skull which put the origin of man back by one and a half million years. This was particularly dramatic because the earliest skull previously discovered had been found by his mother, Mary Leakey, in Olduvai Gorge in Tanzania a few years before; an extraordinary family record.

We could not have wandered about as much of the world as we had without becoming fascinated by the subject of Early Man – this led to Ralph's novel *Levkas Man*, and while researching this we had spent a memorable winter exploring the caves of the Dordogne.

So, naturally, we hoped very much to meet Richard Leakey while we were in Kenya. But, in the first excitement of his sensational discovery, everyone in the world seemed anxious to meet Richard Leakey. As he was sorting out the reverberations of his 'find' (including some violent personal attacks from colleagues who didn't like their previous assumptions being upset), and as he had recently been made Curator of Nairobi Museum (also a subject for attack, on grounds of his youth and 'lack of proper qualifications') he was fending people off hard.

However, a meeting was arranged, and in his office at the Kenya National Museum in Nairobi we talked across his big desk, and were allowed to see and hold the skull. Richard pointed out the very large brain capacity – 800 cc, while modern man's averages 1400 cc. The sections fitted so perfectly, the gaps were so small. He would not join the two sections, nose and head, as the angle would signify different periods and cause infinite controversy.

'The only, absolute way to silence criticism would be to find another skull like it,' I said, and he answered with absolute conviction, 'I'm sure I shall – and not one, but more than one.'

Sometimes a first meeting 'takes', conversation flows and you are obviously on the same wavelength. When we were about to tear ourselves away, Richard came out with one of the most dazzling and unexpected invitations I have ever received. He suddenly said to Ralph: 'Why don't you bring Dorothy, and I'll bring my wife Meave, and I'll fly us up in my Cessna, and we can spend a family weekend at the camp. Then I can show you the site – you'll see it all, the whole extraordinary area – and we can talk and talk and talk!'

So we met Richard at Wilson Airport outside Nairobi on the morning agreed. Our party consisted of Meave, her ten-month-old baby Louise; Richard's four-year-old daughter by a previous marriage, Anna. And a magnificently black African called Mac Kamoya (who made a wonderful picture playing with the very blonde Louise!). He was chief assistant, 'It's always the Africans who find the best things, they seem to have an instinct.' Richard had thrown in his lot with the future of Kenya – how could he do otherwise, when his life-work was buried in the soil of Kenya? He told us he had as many black friends as white – 'more'.

The little plane was packed with food and drink, things for the children, finally the people, and we took off. Richard told us he had qualified as a pilot because he had been nervous of flying, and felt it was a weakness he should conquer. Now he enjoyed it, also it was very useful to his work to be independent. He was a good pilot, relaxed but responsible, making radio contact with the ground every hour, as we were flying over some very wild country. Flying low enough to see in detail the bare and savage land as it had been thrown about by volcanic eruptions millennia ago, its loneliness never disturbed since the earth's early cataclysms until violated from the air.

Richard pointed out geological features as we flew over them, making it simple for the layman. Ralph drew small maps for reference. Anna ate an orange. Louise was slightly sick – 'She's always sick when we've just crossed the Equator,' Meave said.

He had always had a strong feeling about this area, Richard told us, particularly the north-eastern shore of Rudolf, near the Abyssinian border. Geologists all told him that it was covered with volcanic ash, which it looked like from the air. Unable to get overland to this remote spot, he went down to it in a helicopter, and found his hunch was right. It was not volcanic ash, but old lake-shore sediments full of fossilised bone fragments which heat, wind-erosion and occasional rainstorms had brought to the surface. So he left the expedition he was with, 'acting as a sort of dogsbody to senior scientists', and returned to the place that so attracted and excited him. Rather like a comet, his direct route to what he wanted left a certain trail.

Four years of work and struggle followed; endless, meticulous work in the exhausting heat; and always, too, the effort his father Louis had always had to make, the effort to interest the outside world in what he was doing so as to raise sufficient funds to continue.

At the beginning of our flight we had flown over the Aberdares, which we had recently crossed by Land Rover. We saw the Saguta Valley, considered the hottest place in Kenya, full of geysers and hot springs. Once it had been a part of Lake Rudolf, until lava pouring down from Mount Kulal formed a plug and sealed it off. Then we saw Rudolf again, hazed with heat, and looked down on South Island which we had circumnavigated. Then for the first time we saw the other two islands in this long, long lake, Central Island and North Island.

We flew down to a spit of land, jutting out into the lake just before North Island. This spit is called Koobi Fora, 'the place of sand'. We came to rest on level sandy ground patterned with scrub, and realised a very large camp was spread along the lakeside. Now it was empty except for a handful of people to look after it. At their time of maximum activity it had held more than seventy. A few Topi and some Grant's gazelles were grazing near the runway; they lifted their heads to glance at the familiar plane, then went on grazing. Two men came out to help unload the stores. The heat wrapped round us like damp flannel as we walked over the sand to our hut.

Reed-thatched, the huts had half-walls to allow air to circulate. Sandstone slabs form the floors, and also make a path down to the water. In the communal mess tent, Richard poured us all a cold (soft) drink before lunch, while Meave and Anna sat on the step picking over a tray of fossil fragments. Louise was cooing naked in a tin bath. One side of this long hut was all bookcase – this was a home as well as a place of work. Meave has a Ph.D in Zoology, specialising in bones. Richard made a very charming speech about how her work before marriage made her so valuable to his work now, as well as the pleasure of shared enthusiasm.

A few small boats were drawn up on the shore, but the Africans waded in chest-deep to catch tilapia and borous with a seine-net, apparently confident they would see a crocodile before it saw them. Indeed, everyone bathed, and the children played at the edge of the water. There were hippo pug-marks on the shore – the camp had its personal hippo, who liked to play with an empty petrol drum and chain used as a mooring. Once he tore it loose, and was discovered in the morning asleep, cuddled up to his toy. Richard thought he was an adolescent in need of affection. The camp rose to a slight ridge, and on its peak was the lavatory-hut. We asked why it was positioned in the place of honour, where the church tower would stand in an English village. Richard said, 'Because I like the view from there.'

He warned us to take a torch if we left our hut during the night, as there were armed guards about the camp after dark, and to shine it on the ground to establish identity – also to scare off scorpions. Prince Philip's secretary (I think they had been the only previous non-scientific guests) forgot this, and felt the muzzle of a rifle against his back before he had heard any sound or movement. The guards were probably a wise precaution, as we'd heard the general opinion that Richard was in considerable danger at Koobi Fora from the Shifta – raiding bands from over the Abyssinian border. He denied this. We also saw lion pug-marks about the camp in the morning. I asked Richard how the night guards and the lions shared out the territory; he said he'd sometimes wondered about that, but was waiting till he heard.

When the heat had abated a little, we went in the open Land Rover to the most recent fossil site, and fell at once into the palaeontologist's occupational deformity; stooping forward with eyes raking the ground. Recent rain had exposed the bones of antelope, hippo, crocodile. One sensed the infinite patience necessary to search and search and search, led on by hope of the blinding moment when you pick up a fragment that might make history. One girl who had worked with them had a Topi form a strong attachment to her, and accompany her everywhere – waiting for her in the morning and moving beside her through the long, slow, monotonous days of searching.

I remember Richard standing beside a wall of strata which was in layers like a cake, and showing us just why there was so much to be found here. Over millions of years the layers, and everything deposited in them, had piled up like mille-feuilles pastry. But weather conditions had shifted it till the layers were spread out on the surface like a pack of cards. So the bones of Topi who had grazed here in prehistoric times lay on the ground where Topi grazed today (the physical structure of the animals had in many cases changed remarkably little judging from the piles of their bones discarded outside the mess hut).

But it was not till the next morning that we were taken to the site where the famous skull had been found. We went in the Cessna and the flight took ten minutes. 'That's why we use aircraft, by Land Rover it's four and a half hours.' We landed on a little strip that had been cleared of thorn bushes. Mac Kamoya disappeared over a rise, to search an area on his own. Richard led us over the sandy hillocks till we came to a concrete post with a number on it. 'This is where we found it.' A thick layer of volcanic ash had preserved the skull, and this had eroded very slowly, leaving it on the surface. They hoped still to find tiny fragments that were missing; the carefully sifted trays Meave had been examining back in camp had been brought from here. The danger now was that tourists, following the great publicity, would start chartering planes and flying up to see the place, and tramping over it might disturb and destroy things of value. So the government had given Richard protection for two thousand square miles. This, it was hoped, would become the great new Game Reserve of Eleret.

The discovery of the skull had really been accidental, they had been searching for artefacts! But since then, they had found remains of both Homo and Australopithecus at the same level – these two, the carnivorous Homo and the herbivorous Australopithecus living at the same time. Another disturbing bombshell of a question mark to launch into accepted thought! As another palaeontologist said to us later; 'When finds are few, theories are easy, everything's nice and tidy. Leakey's find makes everything more complicated.'

He was still urgent to find very early artefacts, so establishing that the extraordinary brain capacity of the skull had been expressed in achievement, and was not a freak, diseased head as had been suggested!

He stooped, brushing the sand from a greenish-looking stone. Stones of that colour (denoting kind) were likely to be of interest. He thought it might have been a pebble-chopper. We covered it carefully with flat pieces of rock, so it could be photographed in situ before being moved, and marked the spot. Everything must be provable, as everything would be questioned.

It was strange to scramble about in the heat picking up bits of bone or stone, childishly asking 'Is this anything?', and to know that one might, one just might ... ! Very compulsive.

But, as always to me, it is at night that the character of a place establishes itself most strongly. (Even one's own garden, I find, is different at night – a little wild, belonging to itself, stirring from human domination.) And Africa always pressed in most strongly during the blessed cool of the evening drink before dinner, sudden dark having taken the country. Especially, of course, at Koobi Fora. The place has a very strange atmosphere. Other places are older, but they don't emanate geologically what this northern shore of Lake Rudolf does.

We sat for drinks outside our hut, as there was a big verandah, Richard, Meave, Mac, Ralph and I. It was quite dark and there was no moon, but the curve of the ground beyond which lay the site where we had scrambled and searched was just visible against the stars. All light had passed from the water. Long lost to sight were the Goliath herons who had stood, as still as heraldry, one on each spit of land, fishing for their supper.

Could it really have been here, as Richard believes, that the earliest of our kind first began to grope about their earth? It is a very strong and secret place, but at night it has a strange sense of opening. As if it pushed time away, and we five sitting in the dark were connected with the early people; as the Topi we had seen grazing this afternoon were one with the animals who had once animated those discarded bones.

During our visit Richard said: 'When you're in Tanzania, you must go and see my mother ... I've written to tell her you're coming, she's expecting you!'

Some time later, in the Serengeti, we drove along the edge of the great plains to the ford that crosses the Olduvai River, up towards the Ngorongoro Crater, then swung left towards the Gorge that Louis and Mary Leakey had made famous throughout the world. With every mile of wilderness we covered, it seemed less and less probable that Richard could have got a letter to his mother from Nairobi, and we felt very diffident about invading this unknown and famous lady. We knew of the colourful and eventful life she had shared with Louis. What would she be like, continuing their work alone now since his recent death, working and mentally living in the remote past?

The Gorge where the finds of early man were made is now something like a tiny reserve, the entrance manned by an African warden. We drove on up a stony track that climbed to the top of the Gorge, and came upon a house, so remote it might have been dropped out of the sky, into nowhere. So shaded, and so blended into its background, you didn't see it till you were upon it, and saw someone who must be Mary Leakey coming out to greet us.

Instantly we were at ease, at home. Of course she hadn't had a letter from Richard! The first she'd known of our visit was when she saw the Range Rover coming up the track. But she welcomed us with such a warm and easy charm, this slim, dainty, agile woman who carried with her an air of eagerness, of pleasure: a kind of restlessness.

She had a dark American girl staying with her, who was typing at a table in front of the house, and various African helpers, most of whom had worked with her and her husband for a long time. Over a cold drink outside, she countered our apologies by saying, 'I knew you were here, and were visiting Richard, but I was afraid you weren't coming to see me. I'm stuck on a thesis, it's lovely to have an excuse to take a day off!'

Her house looks across to magnificent views, right over the Gorge, which drops away into invisibility, towards the Ngorongoro Crater. Inside, a big circular sitting-room strewn with mysterious and fascinating objects, but comfortable, pleasant to live in! and two bedrooms, also welcoming, home-like, where sophisticated clothes hanging in open cupboards, and familiar toiletries on the dressing-table, remind one that she was not captive here – she might suddenly ring up from London.

We walked from the house to see her most recent discovery;

a so-far inexplicable network of finger-marked, shallow hollows in smooth rock, linked by channels. Early salt-pans? No one had yet suggested an explanation. It was man-made, and elaborate.

After lunch we drove right down into the Gorge, then walked a long way below the crumbling red cliffs along sandy mounds between clumps of the tall-flowered prickly-leaved sisal which gives the place its name – 'Olduvai' is Masai for 'the Place of The Wild Sisal' – to the site of her historic find; a little stone set in the sand, marked very simply just with her initials, M.L. and the date. She stood thoughtfully beside it, then said with her charming smile: 'Of course, since Richard's find, mine's old hat!'

We were to remember this moment very vividly when, in England, in 1977, we read in the papers that Mary Leakey had found near Olduvai Gorge an even earlier skull, which it was believed might pre-date Richard's by ... was it another million years?

So the Leakey family's game of leapfrog continues.

Their Beards Were White and Their Eyes Were Red

The Migration of the Wildebeest

RALPH HAPPENED to meet Hugo van Lawick on the steps of Collins in St James's Place one day, and told him we were coming to East Africa. 'By February I shall be back in my temporary camp in the Ngorongoro Crater,' Hugo said. 'If you can come to the Serengeti then, you may be lucky enough to see the Great Migration. Let me know when you're coming, through George Dove on Lake Ndutu. I keep in touch with him and we can meet up.'

When February came, and we returned from the Northern Frontier District to Nairobi, and news of other places, we heard that the rains in Tanzania had been very late, that the Serengeti was under water, and the wildebeest were dropping their calves into puddles. But we had already been several months in East Africa, and we had plans to go to South Africa before we returned home. It was now or never. We sent a message to Hugo (the curious grapevine that operates between the isolated and colourful personalities of the animal-world in Africa informed us he was back) and we set out again with Jonny Baxendale in the blue Range Rover.

It is more tactful to cross the frontier from Kenya to Tanzania at some places than at others – the formalities are more straight-forward – and this we did.

The Serengeti is one of those patches of the earth's surface which have taken character from the people who have loved it, served it, written about it ... Dr Grzimek who said 'Serengeti shall not die' and his son who was killed trying to make that come true. The rolling lion-coloured plain seems to stand for all that is left of a world teeming with lives undisturbed by humans. Here the immemorial groups still live side by side in their quiet sensible way. Whereas in the N.F.D. each animal had been a discovery, here there was a constant profligacy of creatures. Groups of lions in the air-conditioned position, lying on their backs with their legs in the air. The long necks of giraffes sprouting through the branches of a tree, and then moving off, large and small, with a dreamlike beauty of motion as if they were making their way through water. The surprisingly hand-some head of a hyena (only his mean hindquarters spoil him) poking up from a culvert under the road, which was his home. The great shapes of elephants standing so still under trees, they form gradually to the eye out of sunshine and shadow. The light-foot shy gazelles lifting their heads to any rumour of scent. They often graze near giraffe, knowing these tall creatures will see any approaching danger first.

The road to George Dove's camp on Lake Ndutu was to become familiar as only a road home becomes; night after night through the trees, beside the lake. Half-hutted, half-tented, it had grown beyond all recognition from the lonely small begin-nings, and was now the base camp for the Serengeti.

We drove over the great plain, at first along a rutted track, then none. We became familiar with the group of rocky out-crops, like Kopjes, standing out from every direction as islands stand up from the sea, marking a stage on every outward or homeward journey. Leopards like to lie up in these rocks, I was told, and looking round carefully for a leopard one day when I dropped off at one of these outcrops, I was set upon by a swarm of the terrible black bees of Africa – far more hostile than any leopard! I was so frightened, I ran back to the Range Rover without even doing up my clothes, clawing at my face and neck with the things still buzzing round me, and Jonny pulled out each sting very carefully, dead straight, to make sure of getting the root. I put on anti-histamine cream, and calamine on top of that, and took an anti-histamine tablet – everything I could think of – and all was well, though the area of each sting remained quite hard for several days.

I sometimes envy Ralph's extraordinary gift of memorising country as he passes through it, and his navigator's knack of relating map to actual place, so that at the end of any day he can remember the phases of a journey in accurate detail. But there are compensations, and to me places of great character have mystery and magic just because the detail is blurred. An impressionist view certainly, sometimes almost an abstract, everything reduced to a pattern.

We visited Hugo. I could not map the Ngorongoro Crater, but I remember the apparently endless steep bends of the road climbing up to its rim, and the sense of discovering a remote and secret land as one first looked down into that enormous saucer. Then down, down on the inside of the rim.

Hugo emerged from among undergrowth like any other bush-dweller from his hidden lair – 'Yes, we had to cut the long grass back a bit round the camp, we found a lion between us and the loo,' said one of the two students who were with him.

He had recently finished his film *The Wild Dogs of Africa*, the first of his award-winning films, already shown twice across America, and being shown in England at this time. 'They're back, the Genghis Pack,' he said. 'It might be possible for you to see them.' The Genghis Pack was the name he had given to the particular tribe of wild dogs he had studied so long and carefully. Nomadic within a given area, like so many wild animals, they had apparently circled back and been seen on the plain not far from George Dove's camp, where someone kept watch on Hugo's behalf. Only he knew each member of this group by sight – roughly a dozen – but it was probably them as it was unlikely another group would invade the Genghis Pack's territory. 'I'm going out to try and see them. I want to see how the group may have changed since we finished the film, who's come, who's gone, how they all are. If I find out where they are, I'll let you know, and you might like to come out with me one evening to see them.'

I asked him if the film was a documentary or if he'd built it into a story. 'The story happened,' Hugo said, and told me in detail how the personalities of the wild dogs became clear, and their relationships interacted, building up their own story, during the long time he watched them. 'They got so used to my Land Rover they barely noticed it,' he said. 'It became just a part of the landscape, they paid no attention.'

Later, on the Serengeti, we watched for the Genghis Pack one night, sitting quietly in our vehicles, looking over the rough empty ground as night fell. I didn't know how or where they might manifest themselves – or, indeed, quite what they were like. But it grew dark, and they did not come.

I was shocked when Jonny mentioned casually to the driver of a vehicle we met on the way home, that we had been with Hugo van Lawick watching for his wild dogs. I felt instinctively that the whereabouts of any wild animal must be kept secret from human intrusion, which always imperils it in some way.

The ten square miles of the Ngorongoro Crater seemed like an imaginary painting of the world when young – totally undisturbed, remote, secure, an infinite variety of animals living and moving about in acceptance of each other, many varieties visible at the same time, as if laid out in some impressionist picture of creation. This was something outside time. (Will time catch up with the Ngorongoro, and man invade it?)

On the way out a black rhino challenged us beside the lake. We had to pass him to reach the road up out of the crater. Jonny drove the Range Rover in a wide semi-circle, always avoiding direct confrontation, only accelerating when the centre of the semi-circle was reached, and speed would take us away from the rhino, not towards him. He followed for a bit, but not far.

By a miracle of good luck, the great migration had begun as we arrived in the Serengeti, continued for about a week, and when we left the plain was empty. I knew that every year many people came from all over the world to see this unique sight, one of the great natural spectacles, and could be disappointed again and again.

Following the small rains new grass springs, and the herds move down from the bush country of the north and west to graze the newly-green plains and to calve. No one can set a date for this irreversible annual surge of more than a million animals. It is chiefly wildebeest who are on the move, but there are also many zebra. The predators – lions, hyenas, jackals, wild dogs, – gathered for this potential food, seem caught up in the overall movement like stones over whom a tide rolls. Day after day the horizon was lumpy with black dots which were the backs of wildebeest. I had imagined this famous migration to be some sort of stampede with urgent, excited animals plunging forward in a mass. Nothing could be more different. They wander calmly, with the gentleness which is the character of the wildebeest, in groups and skeins of varying numbers, each group full of recent calves, miraculously able to keep up within a few days – hours, even – of their birth. They graze as they go, though the grass is now short and brown, swinging their great heads to glance sideways with their perpetually anxious look, frisking their thin tufted tails, so at variance with their massive, shaggy fronts.

The numbers seem inexhaustible, unending. Strewn among them are parties of zebra, breaking the pattern with their shiny stripes – always looking so sturdy and plump and well. For a week we lived in the midst of this army on the move. As far as the eye could reach, in every direction, the plain was in motion, waves of wildebeest moving like a sea.

Driving over the plain, we were constantly changing course to avoid large concentrations of animals, weaving between the smaller groups, anxious not to drive and hurry them with so many young calves. (We had heard of tourists urging minibus drivers to chase the animals so they could get good close-up photographs to take home.)

Returning home at night, groups of wildebeest were always sweeping across our track, turning their heavy heads to look towards us with their perpetually worried faces, lumbering on with a curious air of startled haste. As their bodies disappeared in the quick-growing dark, only the white beards under their chins still showed. Catching the headlights they glowed luminously – endless bunches of pale little lamps crossing in front of us. Then even that was lost, and only their eyes gleamed very red, always turned towards us, batches of disembodied red eyes.

Hugo arrived at Dove's camp and said he had located the Genghis Pack. He thought we might see them, perhaps see them set out on a hunt. 'It's some time since they've eaten, I think they'll have to hunt tonight.'

We set out to keep this strange assignation in Jonny's Range Rover, following Hugo's Land Rover out across the plain. We stopped, it seemed to me, at nowhere in particular, the Serengeti needs navigating like an ocean, and settled down to wait.

To my incredulous horror, no less than seven minibuses full of tourists drew up in a line near us. Hugo's 'eyes', whoever he was, had been very helpful to the tour organisers staying at Dove's camp, telling them of the possibility of this exciting and unexpected entertainment. They called to each other through the windows from bus to bus, got out to exchange film, played their radios. Hugo was plainly uneasy. After a time, he asked the drivers of the minibuses to explain to their passengers that if they hoped to see anything they must keep quiet, and this slowly took effect. Finally everyone was silent and still.

The first shadow dimmed the long glare of the day. Still we waited as the endless plain subtly changed colour. Suddenly a wild dog appeared to rise up out of the ground, quite near us, stretched itself, yawned. Then another, and another, a whole line of them rising out of the coarse tufty grass. How had they been concealed? In shallow hollows in the ground, I learned later.

After a general stretching and sniffing, the dogs began to greet each other. Suddenly the whole line was in motion, a tumultuous manifestation of newly-awakened energy, where a few minutes before there had been no sign of life. Each dog has to greet every other dog with an enthusiastic tail-wagging, running to-and-fro in a ballet, a chain-dance of delighted recognition, weaving and intermingling. As the life of each dog depends on the group, I imagine it is their interdependence and need for solidarity which are expressed in this punctilious formality of each saluting each before the night's work begins. The dominant male and the dominant bitch are the first to give greeting; on their decisions and leadership the unknown hazard of the night's quest for food will mainly rest.

As suddenly as they had started, they stopped, dropped into the ground again, and completely disappeared. After a brief pause they emerged again and repeated the greeting ceremony, but more perfunctorily, in a hasty token way. Then they stood around, scenting the air, obviously making up their minds. Which way to go? Which direction promised best? Several of them came up to the Range Rover, lifting their heads and sniffing. The concentration on scent, and the comparative unimportance of sight (as in domestic dogs) gave some of those faces lifted to us almost a blind look. I had never seen heads like that before. Less beautiful than the dingo, variations of dark brindle in colour, they have a hound-like look. Old tapestries show dogs not too unlike these wild ancestors of so many.

After milling around for a bit, they seemed almost imperceptibly to reach an agreement on which way to go. They did not form a pack, as I had imagined hunting animals would, it was all much more haphazard. They set off in a straggling line, but in a quiet way there was something implacable about it, a sense of necessity and purpose. Spread out like beaters, they commanded the widest range of scent or sound.

This was the moment when I had presumed we and the other humans would have the decency to go home. Those animals should be allowed to pursue their imperative, age-old business in mystery and the dark.

Not so. Jonny driving us, and the seven minibuses full of tourists, all revved-up and set off in pursuit. The dogs' effortless gait was surprisingly fast, and they were attuned to the uneven surface of the plain over which motor vehicles bumped wildly, as it was now too dark to see minor rocks and craters. I had never before realised what blood lust is. Nothing could have stopped those cars. I screamed, 'No, no, stop. We don't want to follow them, it's disgusting, leave them alone, we've no right to follow just to watch, it's their business.' No one took any notice. We drove wildly, dead straight over all obstacles, following the pursuing dogs; even the heavy Range Rover jumped and slithered. I remember nearly sobbing with rage, 'I'm ashamed to be here, ashamed of us all, we're as bad as the bloody tourists, this isn't our business, leave them alone, let them go.' I felt caught up in an uncontrollable stampede. This pack of humans wanted to watch someone else's kill. In them was the heat and excitement totally lacking in the quiet purposeful dogs. I had a violent sense of intrusion, as if we were committing an outrage – nasty voyeurs at something which belonged to the Serengeti and the night . . . .

The darker it got the more violently the vehicles careered, jerking round obstacles only visible at the last moment. We stopped when the dogs stopped, at a small straggle of zebras. We were near Hugo's Land Rover. He alone had a right to be here, shadowing them with care and knowledge, he had become part of their lives. He had made millions of people all over the world interested in these dogs, spent more than a year of his life studying them. He had a creative purpose. It was the rest of us who had no right to be there.

The dogs circled and wove, always in that seemingly casual, haphazard, unemotional way, but one realised they were working to cut two zebras off from the rest. They cooperated with skill and patience, until there were two zebras who could not rejoin their group, which disappeared. The dogs were all

round them, manoeuvring purposefully. The two zebras stood
side by side, only moving to face any dog that came in nearer.
But they stood. The dogs tried to shift them, to startle them into
flight. If the zebras lost their nerve and ran, the long chase
would be on and in the end the dogs would bring down the
weaker. Some of the dogs might be injured by the zebras'
hooves, but they would probably get one. If there had been only
one zebra, the dogs might have risked attacking. But not two.
They're big animals, and kick hard.

Later, Hugo said he thought they were probably mother and
son. The young one could have made off before the dogs closed
them in, and they would have settled for the one that was left.
But he said he was not surprised at their standing by each other.
Zebras form very strong attachments to each other, he had seen
other instances ... once a lame zebra with a fit companion
staying by him and out-facing a predator.

Gradually the dogs drew further off, their purpose shifting.
Because the zebras didn't run, they had saved themselves. The
dogs gave them up and set off again, their scattered formation
barely distinguishable against the ground.

They found wildebeest, and very quickly isolated one with a
small calf. Possibly it was too young to keep up with its herd.
Newly-born wildebeest calves are the chief food of all the
predators in the Serengeti at this season.

The seven minibuses swung smartly into place and drew up
in a straight line away to our right, quite close to the animals.
To our left Hugo's car sidled up slowly and merged into some
sort of cover. The wildebeest stood over her calf, her great head
lowered, watching the circling dogs, trying to keep an eye on
them all. The dogs worked slowly, settling down to their contest,
knowing a swipe of that heavy head could kill them. There was
no trace in their bearing of ferocity, savagery, rage – any of those
violent things I had imagined hunting predators would show
their quarry. They were as matter-of-fact as housewives shopping, using their built-in judgement and patience and skill to get
this necessary meal, knowing the big animal who could cripple
or kill them must be out-manoeuvred or driven off or tired

out before they could eat. They had already been baulked once tonight. Predators seldom choose to kill during full darkness, the last of the light and the first of the light are their time.

Every now and then one of the dogs sprang in towards the calf, snapping at it. The wildebeest never knew from which direction the attack would come, and to repel it she had to dart towards it, leaving the calf unprotected. She was incredibly careful not to catch it with her hooves in stepping over it, but once at least she did catch it a glancing blow. After each advance to fend off a dog she instantly drew back to her defensive position over the calf, which appeared to move very little. Perhaps its small movements were difficult to see as all the time the light was fading, and one's eyes were riveted by the constant uncertainty as to which dog would leap in; towards which side – or behind her – the circling wildebeest would plunge to drive it off. As she lunged towards one dog, another would come in from the other side and try to tear at the calf. At last, surely, the calf was not moving at all? But one could hardly even distinguish the small dark heap. Every now and then, whenever she dared to take her eyes off the dogs, the wildebeest would drop her head and sniff at it, nuzzle it enquiringly, trying to find out how it was.

The dogs' attacks followed each other more quickly now, and the wildebeest hardly had time to turn from one to the next. More frequently one of them got under her guard and reached the calf for a second before she drove it off. It became too dark to see the dogs, only the constantly moving head of the mother was still visible – lowered, raised, turning as she made the nimble jumps forward and back, towards an attacking dog, back to stand over her calf. She was now in constant movement; curiously dainty, precise movements for such a lumbering animal.

Then even she was lost into darkness. The entertainment over, the minibuses revved up and roared off home, and a few minutes later Hugo moved off and we followed him.

'She'll realise in the end that that little thing isn't going to get up and follow her again,' Jonny said. 'Then she'll draw off and leave it.'

Later, Hugo came and talked to me about it. I was inexperienced, he most deeply experienced in the life and behaviour of the Serengeti, but he was as amazed as I was. 'I've never known anything like it,' he said. 'It was quite incredible, that she should fight them off for so long. Usually it's over very quickly – a few seconds.'

I asked him if he thought the presence of so many vehicles had affected the way the animals behaved. 'Oh yes,' he said, 'it must have done. Anything different or strange always affects the way animals behave. Even the dogs – they seemed uncertain, lacking in confidence. As for that wildebeest!'

'Do you think in some vague way she felt that because there were other things present, there might be some interruption, some distraction which would help her, might turn to her advantage, and that's why she went on?'

'It's possible,' Hugo said. 'I've known an animal at bay actually come and press itself against the Land Rover, definitely using it, or trying to use it, in its defence. Anything different changes normal behaviour. Certainly it did tonight. It was fantastic.'

We had often noticed a solitary wildebeest hovering around a small bloody skeleton when we were setting out at the beginning of the day, and thought, 'One of the night's small tragedies.' But the next morning we did not go back to see if the one we knew was still lingering near her arena. Did anyone?

73

Part II

PAPUA NEW GUINEA

Land of Misty Heights

AM I SORRY for them, those naked brown women walking, always walking (always talking), through their land of misty heights? I don't think so. What are they talking about? They are so tremendously alive, so animated, with a thin, hard, muscular vitality. They are not a beautiful race, either men or women. Naked except for a bunch of leaves back and front suspended from a folded strip of material, and in the women's case, the *bilum* bag, always slung round the neck to hang between the shoulders, to carry baby, vegetables, anything.

We went with an Australian Patrol Officer to a remote clan in his area of the Highlands, to bring out three women who were

very ill; one looked as if she were dying. I squirmed as the Land
Rover jumped and jerked and braked over the terrible road
round the mountain, and when we reached the hospital (a
group of huts in open country), I wondered how they had stood
it, and jumped out to help them down. I was just in time to see
a strong thin brown hand hesitate fractionally (she had never
been in a vehicle before) then grip the edge, and a brown leg
shoot out and they were all down, and walking in a little group
into the hospital – talking. This condition and use of the body
as a tremendously efficient instrument, even in mortal illness, is
something that we have not only lost, but forgotten.

We had approached Papua New Guinea through Bougainville, the largest of the Solomon Islands, lying in the South
Pacific just below the Equator; legendary home of headhunters,
cannibals, war canoes. Val Duncan (now, sadly, dead) had
invited us to visit his copper mine on Bougainville. It is the
second largest in the world, virtually dominating the island, and
had imposed some of the most modern technology on one of the
most primitive places. Flying in from Australia to the little
airport of Kieta, we were met by Simon Bonga, a very tall, very
black man who had just been promoted senior PR to Bougain-

ville Copper. Until the previous week he had been assistant PR to a white Public Relations Officer. But the Independence of Papua New Guinea was imminent, and the Australian administration, who had controlled the country since 1946, were replacing white men by local men wherever possible. As he drove us to the hotel Simon Bonga answered all our questions very helpfully and in beautiful English. He himself came from New Britain, the long curving island that lies between Bougainville and Papua New Guinea. At the Davora Hotel, we found a hire car waiting. Ralph had, as always, ordered this in advance, finding it frustrating to be dependent on other people's transport. (It was supposed to have air conditioning, but this didn't work.) In it we explored. We became very familiar with the coast road from the hotel to the town, Arawa – sea on one side and steeply rising rain forest on the other. The road was always deep in puddles and sprinkled with large croaking frogs – not easy to drive between them but I think, like London pigeons, they saved themselves. The frequent downpours were short so that you arrived in the dry more often than you would expect.

The mine manager kindly gave a dinner party for us the night we arrived, to meet the many interesting and varied people concerned with running Bougainville Copper. The meal was planned in a garden as an *Amumo*, or *Hangi* – buried food. The meats and vegetables had been arranged in a big hole in the ground some hours before with hot stones below and above, then the earth put back to keep the heat in. Unfortunately the pouring rain had so cooled the stones that the food would not cook. This did not spoil our pleasure; everything was so new and so many people to talk to. When dressing for the evening the first priority is to cover up – high neck, long sleeves, long skirt or trousers as protection against mosquitoes.

Bougainville Copper had flung a highway up the mountains, it soared in great sweeps through rock and forest from Arawa at sea level to Panguna at the top. Natural regeneration was fantastic. The hillsides blasted for the passage of the road three years before were already covered in young trees. Up at

Panguna they had moved a village, scrupulously re-housing everybody rather better than before; but people don't always like being moved. It was surface mining and the chief fauna of this invading world were the grey trucks moving slowly everywhere like giant wood-lice. They carried the rock to the crushing plant which shook the shed that housed it; or else they carried the tailings (the sludge left when the minerals had been extracted). The volume of tailings posed a great problem – what to do with it? A very creative and practical solution had been found; it was channelled in a concrete sluice right down the mountainside and then deposited round the coast to form artificial islands. One of the most interesting days we spent at Bougainville was with the agronomist, going through the many glasshouses in which he showed us the various plants he was experimenting with in order to discover which would best clothe the new islands – and preferably provide food crops.

Up at Panguna we lunched in the mineworkers' canteen – a large, light, modern building. The cold table was, I think, the finest, most varied and delicious I have ever been loosed on. There was also a long table of hot dishes, a line of men moving steadily along it to be served. They had this fabulous repast twice a day. The management were Australian, New Zealand, occasionally British. The work force, in addition to Bougain-villians, came from Port Moresby, New Britain, Papua New Guinea; and also from the Highlands of PNG. Any trouble was always said to start with the Highlanders – and shortly after we were there, there was very serious trouble; so serious that we read in the English papers of a mob armed with stones surrounding the administration office building. No one seemed to understand them. Indeed, I did not meet anyone at Bougainville who had been up to the Highlands to try and find out. The Personnel Manager said to me, 'A man can be very important to us, very responsible, in a senior position. But unless he goes back to his village at certain intervals, he falls behind with something they call "pay-back", and becomes just what they call a rubbish-man at home. I admit I can't understand their system.' The Highlands, the Highlanders, kept recurring in conversation, always as something puzzling, potentially dangerous.

A new harbour had been built by Bougainville Copper, to receive their supplies and export their minerals. The Harbourmaster took us round it in a small tug; his boatman, a Bougainvillian, whom he regarded highly, was a Seventh Day Adventist. As the day he had off for Service each week was different from everyone else's day off, the Harbourmaster's schedule had to be arranged accordingly.

We flew for the weekend to Buka Island with the English PR and his wife (Simon Bonga had been his assistant, now their positions were reversed). We met at the airport, but the Fokker Friendship failed to take off as they couldn't start the starboard engine; after some delay a Cessna was produced from somewhere. Then they got the Fokker Friendship going and we all got into that. The pilot was a fan of Ralph's, so instead of flying the direct route, he flew us close alongside the volcano of Bagana and around the higher volcano, Balbi. Then a long sweep over the grass landing fields, and we looked down over busy, historic Buka Passage which separates Bougainville from the low island beyond. We landed into greater heat than we had found on Bougainville and took a bus belonging to a formidable Cantonese called Wong Yu. He had been there all his life, including the war, through successive waves of Japanese, Germans, Australians, finally Americans. I don't think he liked the war being mentioned. You'd have needed to be a quick mover to keep on the winning side, but there must have been good pickings in those chaotic times. Then we crossed the Buka Passage in the Government ferry, the *Bougainville Chief*, to the island of Sohana. The Buka Passage is a confusion of colour and voices, boats and people, everything moving, everyone making a noise. The Buka girls are perhaps the most beautiful I have ever seen; very dark with a bloom like black grapes on their skin. The shape of their faces is as harmonious as the lines of a flower. They are tall, quite Junoesque, and seem to fall unconsciously into positions of perfect grace. The men have the same colour and are well proportioned, but the women rivet the eye.

The house we stayed in, Bukalama, had been the District Commissioner's house and we climbed through once beautiful gardens in the usual rain. The house was run as a guest house, but there were seldom any guests, it was in the shabby slide towards disintegration. Sitting on the wide verandah looking over lawns and dripping trees to the water, eating in the huge dining-room, ours the only table used, bathing in the rust-stained bath, one felt all purpose and confidence had gone. One way of life had ended and nothing new had begun. Sitting on that paint-flaking verandah in a torn deck-chair waiting for the rain to stop, one felt how easy it would be to lie there for ever forgetting how to make an effort, as day drifted into empty day. I heard here an effect of rain I had never heard before; when it is falling on the roof as hard (you think) as possible, suddenly, with an almost mechanical jerk, it switches into a different gear and hits with redoubled strength.

Useless waiting for the rain to stop – we made expeditions by ferry across to Chinaman's Quay on Buka; at least four big general stores (one had a partition built down the middle because the two wives didn't get on), on the other side of the road an open market. One day we drove all round Buka Island; Papuan villages were spread along the high cliffs; we visited one or two, under pretext of asking for a girl called Blandine, whose husband worked for Bougainville Copper. She preferred village life but had just been instructed by her village council to return to her husband in Arawa. A very outstanding headmaster

(Australian) took us over his open campus school where he had 400 boarders. And still it rained – 'Big Fello rain true' – meaning 'this is a real rain, not just a local thunderstorm'. However, we managed to navigate the cross-island road we had been told was impassable, the bridge down and very bad going, driving through endless plantations of copra and cocoa.

The sun came out the morning we left, and everything glittered, and the colour and movement of the packed craft on Buka Passage dazzled the eye. We bought four cans of 'lolly-water' (orangeade) from Mrs Wong Yu, which we drank as we strolled along the sands looking at the reef, and waiting for our aircraft to come in. So back over speckled blue water and under the cloud galleons to Bougainville. We found a telephone message from Port Moresby, our next destination – an extraordinarily kind and happy message, as it turned out. It was from the British Commissioner of Papua New Guinea to say he had 'taken the liberty of cancelling your hotel booking', as he hoped we would stay with him and his wife at Moresby House. This was not only extremely pleasant, but began a lasting friendship.

Flying away from Bougainville we looked down on the familiar mine buildings, the great grey river of the tailings; then a long passage over empty sea, flying south-west, then crossed the long thin peninsula which Papua New Guinea throws out between the South Pacific and the Coral Sea, and so down into Port Moresby – named for the young English naval Lieutenant Moresby, who had first discovered it in 1873.

In Port Moresby the heat seemed an attack which one could not resist. Outside the beautiful air-conditioned house, with its breathtaking views over the town to the Coral Sea; or the air-conditioned car our host so kindly lent us, nothing seemed worth making the effort for. Here we found again the problem of a man from the Highlands who had come down to seek employment. The British Commissioner's driver earned enough to pay the $40 air fare to the Highlands, but had a struggle to keep up his status there.

We explored a long teeming village built on stilts (Tatana Island), where dug-out canoes were being carved on the quay among the milling children and dogs. Here was energy, animation, smiling faces, always activity, even the endless cross-bred dogs seemed generally in tolerable condition, and all seemed connected to a specific house – their family.

Our host had quietly arranged everything which, we were to find, would make our time in the Highlands illuminating and real. A visit to the Australian Head of State resulted in his alerting his District Commissioners throughout the Highlands to show us their areas. A dinner party carefully chosen to introduce us to people who could tell us most about the country, from different points of view. Independence should have been celebrated while we were there, but a currency problem delayed the event.

I remember the British Commissioner's house at Port Moresby not only with pleasure and gratitude (I hated leaving that exquisitely appointed bedroom and bathroom in apple green and snowy white), but also with pride. It had been one thing to represent your country and monarch in a faraway place when you had power and wealth behind you and a large staff to run an impressive residence. Quite another now it depended on the personalities of the people. In the present moment of our history I found it moving and memorable that my country should be represented by two people with such outstanding character and sheer style. The morning we left, they had to turn out formally with the other diplomatic representatives to meet the Governor-General at the airport. He was flying in from Australia to tour Papua New Guinea in a ceremonial valedictory visit to mark the end of Australian rule. Our host gave us a lift to the airport, the big car gleaming, the driver gleaming, the Union Jack flying. Our hostess wore a big hat – 'I had to, the sun gives me a headache, though I've spent most of my life skipping back and forth over the Equator.' They both looked classic, with that indefinable unconscious distinction. But he had brought us our morning tea in bed and she had cooked (quite perfectly) the large dish of trout which had been a main course for the dinner party the night before. They had very recently arrived and were not yet unpacked – she was sorting out 'my things', her own silver and china, from what she called 'the Queen's things' – the official appointments of the house. All the help she had was one boy – of a good tribe, very quick and willing, but she had to teach him one thing at a time, every detail being new to him. He had mastered the Hoover, and how to make beds. I found him laying the dinner table impeccably, with rapt concentration, and being naturally deft, he waited at table, which he enjoyed (a ceremony is fun, people are interesting). When our hostess first flickered into the drawing-room, we thought it was either a teenage blonde or a butterfly. One knows these dainty, brittle, Dresden china women who are stronger than any steel. 'This is our third term of service in a very hot, very trying climate,' she told us. 'I'm dehydrated, if I stopped I should never start up again.' There was an injured bird crouched on their drawing-room balcony above the precipitous garden which dropped to the town, and they found time to watch it and give it food and water. 'You can't just pretend he isn't there, or push him over,' our host said. (But the bird died.)

The flight to Goroka, the airport of the Highlands, took off on time, only half full, and we looked down on the great reefs of the Coral Sea and the congested straggle of Port Moresby, which only eighty years ago had been three houses near the beach. The new Government Buildings of independent Papua New Guinea are built seven miles from Port Moresby. We flew up the coast, climbing all the time before turning inwards to the mountains. Looking down over densely wooded slopes, the villages – groups of thatched round huts in circular clearings – looked perfect Noah's ark toys, with tracks and streams shining as tiny threads.

Ralph, as usual, was invited to the flight deck during landing. You can generally get into Goroka; thermals build up, but there are holes in the clouds. It is the sort of informal airport I love. The airport manager waiting for us to come down the gangway said, 'Ah! You've brought a Buka girl, I see!' And turning we saw her, blooming and unmistakable, moving like a queen through lesser people.

We took the Air Nuigini bus to the Bird of Paradise Hotel, and that afternoon we were taken out to see a trout farm by the two young Australians who had started the enterprise. The villagers who worked for them were also shareholders in the farm. It was less revolting than I had expected any intensive farming to be. The sequence of pools as the fish developed from tiny minnows to mature fish were terraced on a rocky hillside using a river. They were not too congested, and the beautiful brown-speckled fish were swimming freely. That day there had been a great slaughter, and a cargo flown down to Port Moresby.

Before going back to Goroka they wanted to visit a village some of their work people came from – there was just time before dark.

We crossed the river and turned off to the left of the track, and saw a group of huts in a clearing. The moment we got out we were immersed in people – black, animated, talking, the children tugging at our hands, the dogs round our feet.

When you have entered a strange country, there is always another frontier to cross; the moment when, with a jerk of excitement, you are involved, when you care about it. This may happen soon or late, but it is as unmistakable as a door opening. For me in Papua New Guinea, it happened in that most relaxed and homelike hour of the day's ending, standing on the trodden grass among the children and dogs, the light going, the dark faces all round us vivid with flashing eyes and teeth, everybody talking; looking into the open huts at the flames of cooking fires and the women bending over them, while the smoke seeped up through the thatch and drifted away like clouds.

The country we had now entered – the Highlands – was a high land of bulky mountains amongst which the cloud always moved, so that the contours of the hills varied from moment to moment, the dark landscape always changing. Dark, because cloud and mist regularly obscured the sun so the mountains were seen in silhouette. In this country there seems no sky; at night you seldom see the stars. Could there be any connection between that and the fact that this is the only country I have ever been in where the people have no religion? – in the widest possible sense, meaning no reaching out to anything beyond themselves? Are they too enclosed, held down to earth by the cloud cover, trapped among their mountains?

It is a country of landslides, the saturated earth always liable to slip and move. It is a country so divided that a very elaborate version of pidgin English is the only language common between the different clans. This pidgin has indeed developed into a language, incorporating many German words (with the word *Kiap* (captain) meaning local boss, still in general use) and some Japanese words incorporated into the basic English. It is spoken extremely fast, so that it is impossible to follow.

We began to make long probes in various directions into this looming, strenuous, very complicated country. Wealth is counted in pigs and the pig fences are as important a part of every village as human huts, perhaps more so. In the north Cassowaries – that huge, untidy, non-flying bird – are also currency. But they have also taken to our currency with enthusiasm. Pausing on the bend of a mountain road to look at the amazing view, we were once overtaken by two men walking back to their village. One, taking a leather wallet from the fold of material holding up his leaves, showed us a very fat roll of banknotes. The Patrol Officer with us, talking to him, thought he was a very lucky gambler, and had won it gambling. 'They do not use banks, but often bury their wealth, so that notes of very old denominations come into circulation from some hoard suspected and searched for, or even dug up by chance.'

The District Commissioner in Goroka asked if we would care to go to a village just north-west of the town, where a meteorite had fallen recently. As it was one of the only five meteorites to have been recovered intact, it had been sent to London for examination, then cut in half. One half was kept for scientific inspection, the other half, beautifully polished and mounted in a red-lined box, was returned to the village, and this the Patrol Officer would formally present to the village council.

We waited in the central open space, while the village Head man called the people in from the fields – that pitched throwing of the voice on a sustained note that carries so far. The call was repeated again and again, and gradually they began to gather. The meeting would have been larger, but some of the men had been on the beer in Goroka the night before, and the riot police had been out. At last, the central meeting space of the village was full and it seemed everyone within earshot had come. Then the Patrol Officer explained what a meteorite was, and what happens when it enters the earth's atmosphere. He spoke in pidgin, too fast for us, but illustrated it with gestures so descriptive even I could understand. The younger people understood pidgin, but few of the older ones did, so a village councillor translated into their language. I was fascinated by an old woman standing by me wearing a woollen cap, and not much else, because every time she moved her head I could see the daylight through a little hole in the side of her nose just beside the left nostril, originally pierced for an ornament I imagine. I don't think she was very interested in the meteorite, she kept looking round at her neighbours. Men listened with interest, sometimes asking a question or making a joke, so there were quick little rounds of laughter. The women made use of the time to examine the children's heads for lice, and when that was done, picked up a dog and removed any ticks, then left the dog lying on their shoulder sometimes, or just holding it. Then one man seemed to make a speech; we learned afterwards he was rather a troublemaker, and was complaining because only half the meteorite had been returned to the village; it had come to them from outer space, so it belonged to them. He didn't get much support; most of them seemed pleased with the nicely-mounted half, and were planning to build a pedestal for it. On the way back to Goroka we passed the men who had been sleeping it off in the gaol overnight, walking home to the village, and they waved cheerfully.

Mission schools in remote places were like islands; a long, fabulous afternoon drive from Goroka ended at a very fine one at Megabo, beyond the upper Bena River. The four-wheel-drive vehicles of the Patrol Officers went like tanks through or over anything – a mountain road, a track, a footpath, or just open country. We seldom drove long without meeting groups

of people walking – men and women, babies in *bilum* bags, dogs
– always animated, always talking. They walked with an air of
eagerness, never a trudge like the people on the roads in Mexico
for instance. The leaves bounced and the breasts protruded. The
women of one tribe had extraordinary breasts – like tubes, no
thicker at the base than at the tip, sticking out at right angles.
They walked fast. Where were they going? 'Well, to market –
at least that's the idea. Or just visiting.' The market was often
no more than a small collection of local produce at a crossroads.
But there the groups who had converged from so many different
directions would sit and talk. It was a social gathering which
lasted all day, as much as a shopping expedition. And when we
returned from some long journey, we would meet the same
groups returning at the end of the day, walking at the same pace,
still talking, *bilum* bags full. Occasionally a man would be
carrying a child, sometimes carrying a dog, and the chatter was
interrupted as they turned and waved and smiled at us. The girls
work in the fields wearing all their finery of beads; wild cane
borders the road.

The saturated ground is always a hazard, and returning from
Megabo, we navigated with care in patches where bulldozers
had left small quagmires; then finally bogged down hopelessly
on the last very narrow concrete bridge over a torrent, where
a truck had cut deep ruts. I found a patch of firm ground to
stand on beside the road while Ralph and the Patrol Officer
examined the situation. I realised we were a long way from
Goroka with no means of getting there. What could we do? We
were also a long way from any village which would give help.
We were on the brink of the short dusk. It was unlikely anyone
would be about so late. I was distracted by the most dazzling
display of rainbows, and sheets of fine rain like silver gauze in
the towering, lowering mountains behind us.

But what would happen to us? I was getting cold – I couldn't
walk for ever on a rocky boggy track in the dark. Anyway, there
was nowhere to walk to. Then, in the extraordinary manner of
some countries, when they appear to be empty for miles,
suddenly people will rise up out of the ground.

I shall always remember the sight of those three people walking abreast down the hill towards us, two men and a woman between them, and – miracle! – the woman carried a spade over her shoulder. They gathered round with much talk and laughter, and after long digging by Ralph, the Patrol Officer, and our rescuers, we managed to nose gingerly out and I could climb back into the Toyota which had again become capable of taking us to Goroka.

A large vigorous man with an aura of personality came into the Bird of Paradise Hotel. He turned out to be Brian McCook, a famous pilot who had brought the first twin-engined Otter aircraft across the Pacific and was now running Goroka airfield. He asked us if we would like to fly out the next day to see two remote and impossible airfields in the mountains. And we made a date, to be at the airfield at 8 o'clock the next morning. As it poured all night I woke wondering how we could possibly fly into such places, or even get off the ground. However, when we arrived at the airport, Brian McCook seemed reasonably optimistic, said we would be off in fifteen minutes, and we were, in a Cessna 185.

We headed for a gap in the ring of mountains that surround Goroka, and it cleared for us just as we reached it. We twisted through narrow passages between mountains, looking down on villages and gardens and pig fences and waterfalls, then slid into

a muddy airstrip in the hills, called Nambaiyupa. Ralph was interested in a wooden-bladed spear a man in the crowd was holding, and Tom Dodd, running the Anglican Mission there, told us that the man had fashioned it slowly, over a long period, probably with one man in mind, the man he meant to kill. It had strangely elongated flat barbs along the blade – a nasty wound. Somehow this spear passed into Ralph's possession, though not at his request. 'But doesn't he value it, having put so much work into it?' Ralph asked. 'He'll make another!' This spear became part of my luggage and I got it safely home.

The Cessna was somehow extricated from Nambaiyupa, found a gap and rose to higher mountains, and ever deepening gorges. And suddenly we saw Onkalai – (described by Jon Cleary in his novel *North from Thursday*), an absurdly steep hill for an airstrip, and a huge crowd to see the plane. Apparently the spectacle never palls, people come in from the villages around and stay all day. Their costumes bridge two worlds. One girl wore a bunch of leaves behind, a beaded sporran in front, both held up by a military style leather belt; on top a nylon blouse, bought from a store in the town. The take-off down that steep hill was immediate. We seemed catapulted over the gorge, the crowd behind us on the ground shrinking to a brightly coloured patch, soon lost. Then we dodged home between mountains and through clouds back to Goroka.

We finally left Goroka in the self-drive Datsun Ralph had hired and set out on our own along the Highland Highway to the town of Kundiawa in the Chimbu country. This meant going over a pass (the Daulo Pass) and the road there was not spoken of too highly. We wound up towards the pass with rock face on the right and a garden of wild flowers on the left. The vivid orange of montbretia dominated continuously, but there were sheets of pale mauve lupins too. Pampas grass that always looks depressingly artificial in gardens, here comes into its own – majestic clumps of creamy plumes springing from black rocks. Beside the Highway children were selling head wreaths of montbretia. As always, the moment you stop people spring out of the ground and press round you – friendly, curious. We stopped in a small town, Asurea, to check our route, and many people asked for a lift. I felt we should take women carrying heavy loads of *kau kau* (sweet potato) and *taro* but Ralph (wisely, as it turned out) took two strong-looking boys, brothers, older teenage I would think, who wanted to get to Watabung. 'Watabung! Watabung!' they said persistently. Ralph remembered the name from the map and it was on the other side of the pass. He thought it might be a good idea to take on some man-power to push in case of need.

Nearing the top we began to find soft patches on the road, treacherous, because sometimes the surface looked all right but was only a crust over softening below from the water pouring down the rocks. Three times I and the boys got out while Ralph manoeuvred, and then got in again, rather muddy, on the far side of the bad patch. Then we stopped again, and as I stepped out I sunk quickly up to my knees. The car had moved out of reach, there was nothing to clutch and I went on sinking – I was terrified. Then the boys, who had found a firm patch, inched back, leaned over, clutched me and pulled me clear. My shoes were lost with a sucking noise. One boy helped me to find a firm patch while the other lay down and, gingerly stretching out, rescued first one of my shoes and then the other. I thought this was wonderful of him, I'd never have dreamed of asking about my shoes, I was too relieved to have been dragged out myself. The car's front wheels were hopelessly bogged, but the back wheels were on something hard and the boys managed to push the car back on to firm standing, from which Ralph could circle the soft patch – just – and find a road again. On the last ascent we stopped to wring ourselves out and clean ourselves up. There was a stream from a little waterfall at the base of the rocks, and I went to it with my mud-clogged shoes. To my great surprise, the boys took them from me and washed them, and also washed my feet before putting them into the shoes again. In a country where, I already realised, the position of women is, to say the least, ambiguous, I was deeply impressed.

The pass itself was all right, and there was only one bad patch on the other side, then a breathtakingly steep descent to Watabung, where the boys left us. It was now very hot. You could see Kundiawa from a long way off, on the opposite hilltop, but the drive there is hard and long. The villages here are all on the top of the hills – right on the crest – the best position to defend; round houses of plaited grass with thatched roofs, gardens of *kau kau* and *taro* running down the hillside, and always the pig fences. The hard-trodden ground between the huts showed yellow.

Kandiawa was black with people when we arrived. Thunder-clouds now blotted out the pass. We had booked a room at the Chimbu Lodge Hotel. This was very pleasant, done up as if for tourists, with flowers and log fires and a big bar. But the people there were not tourists. They were businessmen – commercial travellers with brief-cases and eager expectant faces. Later, a Patrol Officer in another area was to say to us, 'The vultures are gathering for the kill. Waiting for Independence. They're coming in from every country – to get contracts, to get concessions. Lots of slick patter about developing backward countries, from people who don't know the first thing about the country – or care. All they care about is developing backward balance sheets!'

The prospective first President of Independent PNG, Michael Somarez, was widely praised, admired for his integrity, intelligence, the sense and balance of his views. Unfortunately, the majority that brought him to power was a combination of small parties, less solid than the backing of one major group would have been. And rivalries could be sharp. Given time (he was

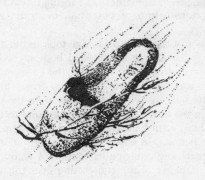

young) and reasonable luck it seemed they could not have started with a better leader.

We had heard much of the Chimbu people, numerous, rich and warlike, and we were now in their country. They had been in a state of war for weeks, and one looked out for smoke to show where a village had been set on fire. This fighting between villages was described to us as more display than aggression. 'They don't play football to let off steam!' The men of two villages, after much talk and preparation, will climb facing hills, yell, charge down and throw an arrow short, throw a spear – short, then retire. This goes back and forth, charge, withdraw, charge, withdraw – great noise and vigour, but out of three thousand to six thousand warriors one may get hurt. Occasionally a girl will advance between the two armies, lift up her *lap-lap* and scream, 'If this is what you want, come and get it if you dare!' – and that really sparks things off. But sometimes villages do get burned. If they've been into a town and got beer then there is real violence. Where there is population pressure, and small numbers with little land to cultivate between the steep rocks, then there can be serious fighting. Strangely, though they all carry axes kept gleamingly sharp, these are never used in fighting, nor are firearms, though there are some about. Only a lot of noise, much ceremonial paint, bows and arrows, and sometimes spears. Occupying their harsh high country among the storms, they seem to maintain a surging threat that seldom erupts; a demonstration of potential, of pride; a need for excitement.

The manager of the Chimbu Lodge took us out to see some caves in which there were mummified bodies, the last placed there only twenty-five years ago. But the road was cut by a landslide. We watched as two bulldozers, driven by Papuans, worked on the bulging side of a mountain-on-the-move. One was digging-in too low, gradually losing ground to the moving earth above him, until he was in danger of being pushed over the precipice below. He was eventually dug out by the contractor's 'digger' and then pulled out by a chain. Then the (Australian) manager of the contracting firm got in the bulldozer himself and worked higher and higher into the slide so it could not fall on top of him. There was quite a collection of vehicles and men coming and going on the wet trampled path. Some had girls with them bringing them Thermos flasks. The path stopped where the brown bulk of hillside had slipped down on to it, near the edge of the precipice, and the bulldozers crawled back and forth, gradually clearing the mass to open the road again. 'Typical of New Guinea,' they said. 'All of the country is on the move all of the time, shifting with the rain, and earth tremors.' They told us that above Daulo Pass quite a few cars got over the top to find there had been a fall on the Watabung side and the road blocked. They would turn and try to get back, only to find there had been a fall behind them and they were cut off. How lucky we had been! A road engineer said, 'Of all the roads built anywhere in the world the Daulo Pass must be the worst. It's heartbreaking the way things move on that last stretch, and they're going on moving.'

On our forays from Chimbu Lodge we scanned the groups we passed on the road for 'Wig Men' – men with the hair of dead people mixed into their own, building up extraordinary beehive shapes.

White people who had lived among the Chimbu for a long time, admitted when pressed that they did not really know or understand them. 'I sometimes wonder if they are doomed to extinction like the brontosaurus; a simple prehistoric subsistence way of life, swamped by the new cash and mechanics.' Did one get this feeling more among the Chimbu than among the other tribes I wondered? – because they were the strongest, would change be more difficult for them?

We left Kandiawa to drive to Mendi. After a few miles we turned off the highway to visit the Assistant District Commissioner at a little township called Kerowagi. The Australian DCs had recently become 'assistant' District Commissioners, the first title being given to Papuans in preparation for the transfer of power. The Australians appeared to be administering their districts as they always had done; the new DCs were to be found in the offices.

At Kerowagi there was talk of the fighting in the area, which had been heavily written up in the press down at Port Moresby. The ADC told us, 'The tribe called the Kumai, who together with the Bandi number about 1400 males, are attacking the Endugwa who number only about 800 males. It appears to be a determined effort to gain territory. It's been going on for more than a year. Ten people have been killed and quite a few wounded, but it's the burning of the villages which is the worst thing; a really big head man had his house burned. It's probably all part of some long distant pay-back or vendetta.' Ralph asked this ADC whether he felt he really understood the Chimbu of his area and he replied, 'Yes, I think I do. But their thought-processes and mine are entirely different. That's the difficulty. That's the block.'

I was longing to talk to the two women we had spoken to briefly as we came through the outer office, and asked if I might. One was white, so we had a common language; the other black. I had not made sense of the position of women in this country; it seemed so contradictory, in behaviour so free and easy and equal. Was it?

The DC's secretary, Judy Penny, started by telling me about the Papuan woman who worked with her, and who had now gone out. 'She's had a sad life, because her husband died of cancer and she was left with two small children. But her husband had worked in this office, so they gave her a job, and now she's secure.' I asked if she thought she would marry again. 'I don't think so,' Judy said. There was 'so far no pressure on her from the head man of her village. And as she's rather educated she'd have quite a lot of Yes and No.' (She had been to a Mission school, and then learned a lot from her husband and from working in this office.)

From this we went on to talking about the marriage customs. 'They like to have a girl baby and not a boy, because the girl gets a big bride-price, and if they can engage her to a rich boy, a boy of a rich family, they can boost the money up and up. Whereas if they have a son they have to save up to pay the bride-price for him when he comes to get married. This is often arranged when they're children – that a girl is to be married to a certain boy, and they have little say in the matter. Yet she is an object of value, which gives her prestige. It's very confused. What is so hard is that when the parents who received her brideprice finally die, they leave it with all their wealth, all their possessions, to their eldest son. She doesn't get any of it, though it was paid for her.'

Judy went on. 'When I told her that in our country the girl receives presents when she marries, that her husband gives her a present, gives her a ring – she thought this incredible, unbelievable! Couldn't understand it.'

I asked her what the actual wedding ceremonies were. 'If they belong to a Mission, of course it's according to that denomination. Otherwise they have a big *Sing-Sing*.'

This word *Sing-Sing* had erupted into every conversation since we arrived in the Highlands. It sounded so jolly and festive, I'd imagined singing and dancing and feasting around blazing fires. Not so. Very gradually we pieced together what this complex ceremony really was and why it is so important.

Money or cash do not establish a man's position. He must use it to buy pigs. Every village has a flat open space which 'might be a *Sing-Sing* ground'. We had seen one *Sing-Sing* ground as long as a rugger field with two houses facing each other on either side. One must have been a hundred feet long. The resident clan would occupy one and the visiting clan would occupy the other. They would not be used again until the next *Sing-Sing*, perhaps five years later. The essential event is a mass pig killing. But they are not eaten – a few may be, but that is not important. It is essentially a display of wealth, wealth expressed in pigs. 'A two- or four-pig man is just a rubbish-man. A rich man can count his pigs in hundreds, perhaps thousands.' The pigs themselves are small compared to ours, and black or darkish. Whoever goes hungry, they do not. They are in fine condition. The country is theirs. But their ending is to be tethered or trussed, and battered to death with clubs. This is the climax of an event that can last for days in mounting excitement and noise as more and more people pour in from all directions, bringing their pigs, to tether and lay them all round the sides of the *Sing-Sing* ground. The *Sing-Sing* establishes the power and prestige of each owner. It is the resident villagers who thus exhibit their wealth, to impress the visiting clan and to repay a debt. The killing is followed by the presentation of the pigs by the resident village to the visiting village. This is the real point of the *Sing-Sing*. The visitors finally take home with them the dead pigs, and some-times living pigs as well (a pig would produce more pigs – so interest accrues). All this will be repaid when the visitors give a *Sing-Sing* in return. The principle is that the more you owe the richer you must be. The more people you are involved with in borrowing and lending, the more you have. 'How rich he must be if he can give away all that!'

'It is as complicated as our stock exchange – rather more so,' the DC said. 'If they earn our money, as many do, they use it to buy pigs and in some districts cassowaries. They are the real sign of wealth. Those two things are the money in the bank, the yacht, the Rolls, the big house – everyone likes his prestige symbol!' But the network of debt and pay-back running on end-lessly, interlocking in all directions, this baffles understand-ing.

We drove on towards Mendi and arrived in a downpour. The pleasant little hotel was run by a Dane. It was quite empty. That day's drive from Karawagi to Mendi imprinted the look of this country on my mind more than any other single day. The endless panorama of bulky mountains blurred with moving mists and cloud; the groups of people along the Highland High-way, always moving fast, the sprays of leaves, picked on the stalk, bouncing up and down on the bare buttocks, usually the fold of material hanging down in front. The women's carriage bent slightly foward under the *bilum* bags, their breasts varying from district to district. Many of the men wore little woolly caps over their frizzy hair, which gave them an almost turbanned look. There is a forward-pressing eagerness about the way these people move. They smile, often wave. Not infrequently, a man will be carrying one of the dogs. Sometimes a stick, sometimes a spear. Beside the road were flowers, some white, some pink, the shape of nasturtiums – mallow? convolvulus? Through the Wangi valley we climbed towards the Hagen ranges. The town of Mount Hagen was crowded, shoppers in a wild mixture of costumes, leaves to nylon – people clothed, half-clothed, un-clothed. *Bilum* bags and plastic bags full of tinned food. Plastic kitchen gadgets. The world's down-market produce. Two people asked Ralph for a job.

Climbing up to Mount Hagen the sun had been scorchingly fierce. We were about 5300 feet up and you add 1500 feet for being so near the Equator. But leaving Mount Hagen, the clouds were closing in on the great Hagen range lying along to our right. The road climbed furiously, and we emerged on to a plateau with the peak of Mount Gilgure (14,000 feet) behind us, and on the other side Mount Lalibu (11,000 feet). The rivers were raging torrents. We entered limestone country, white instead of black. The rain enveloped us. Women in the groups we passed held plastic over the babies on their shoulders, and what appeared to be a large turtle on the move turned out to be a small boy holding a cardboard box over himself. These wet naked women must be cold – it was cold up on the plateau. The pigs were sleek, blue-black in the wet. We passed over bridge after bridge above raging brown water before we reached the straggling town of Mendi.

The Patrol Officer in this district – the old title *Kiap* (Captain) suited him – came from Queensland. He was tall, dark, rangy,

powerful. He had been here for an unbelievable eighteen years. (The first white man had only come into the Mendi valley in 1950.) We stood in the middle of one of 'his' villages. The brown huts, some round, some long, were grouped among Casuarina trees. He stood quite still and talked for a long time while the work and life of the village went on round us. As he talked the life of the place gradually built up like a picture forming out of mist, until we saw them going about their days from youth to age, in sickness and health, happiness and enmity. He told us that here the fighting is real. They do use their axes and their knives. A unit is the family spreading to a clan. The essential of a clan, and why it is wrong to call it a tribe, is that it may not marry within itself, but must marry someone from another clan. The round huts are family units; that big long house to our left was for the men, the one to our right for women – which includes the pigs. Further away there is a separate house for women when menstruating – they don't go to the gardens at all at that time but stay in the house; no work, no responsibility. The children stay with their mothers until the boys are old enough to go into the men's house. He stood silent a moment smiling, then said, 'I must tell you, what I say is true about my people, but the man on the other side of the hill – for his clan everything might be different!'

I think he talked as a deposed king might talk, looking at the kingdom which had been his life, but which he was soon to leave. He expected to go on Independence – 'when he was localised'. Localised – the current phrase on everybody's lips – his job being taken over by a local man. Yes, he could probably stay if he wished, but he didn't want to see everything he had striven for gradually fall apart. 'A Papuan doing my job – it's so much more difficult for him. It's his own country, his own people. He couldn't have the confidence. He might feel exactly as I do about some of the nastier customs – about sorcery, and the slow illness and death that result; about burning down the houses of people you resent – about throwing other clans' babies on the sharp stakes of the pig fences. But it's so much more difficult for him. Whatever his reason tells him, his whole blood stirs with memory and association – he's one of them. Besides, he has a much harder battle to get taken notice of. If I know a man has caused several deaths, I can take him by the throat, shake him till he rattles, and say that if it happens again I'll throw him into prison and lose the key. He knows I won't! But it'll make him think a bit more carefully about the next man he's got it in for. Gradually it won't seem worth it. But a man of the country couldn't do that. Whatever his integrity and motive, it would seem personal, start a vendetta. It's much easier for me.'

He told us he had discussed this matter of sorcery with some of the most intelligent and thoughtful men of the village council, hour after hour, evening after evening, again and again. They came a long way with him in agreeing it was wrong. But they couldn't see a better system. That a man should be 'executed' by the man he had wronged seemed more sensible than handing the quarrel over to strangers – who might reach a wrong decision anyway! 'They simply can't agree that our system is better. This is the one point they can't accept. That they shouldn't kill.'

Here, in the Mendi District, we first saw cassowaries, a row of them in cages that just fitted them, their only possible movement to shoot their heads out between the slats in front. Huge unnatural birds who never fly but run – not fast enough to escape the traps that land them here. Dark blue, ragged long plumage as far as one could see in the dark of the wooden boxes they live in, with reddish purple necks – or are they just raw with rubbing the slats? The families and clans 'ply the Mendi stock market, borrowing on interest, and somehow raising money to buy more cassowaries'.

In another village we were shown a whole rectangle of cages for holding cassowaries. At the moment there were only three birds, but the head man, who had a little English, said repeatedly there would soon be many more. Indicating the empty cages, he kept repeating – wildlife, wildlife. My impression was that they would show how wealthy the village was – but the new label 'wildlife' picked up somewhere would make it more respectable.

Near Mendi we saw several vine bridges. I had heard of these, a narrow bridge woven of vines across a raging stream. Oddly enough it is so skilfully woven and resilient and close-meshed, that it is less terrifying than some more sophisticated bridges I've been on. (I only ventured a very little way.) We watched a house being thatched, much the same as in Suffolk, but with different materials, vines used as ropes. In a four-wheel-drive Toyota truck we drove down limestone cliffs on a road that had been hacked out by hand over innumerable log-edged bridges with slats across, very narrow, over the swollen river. The furthest point in this desperate road – the last place we visited on this patrol – was the high and lonely valley from which we brought the women back to hospital.

At the Mendi Hotel, chatting with the Danish manager, Ralph commented on some extremely strong folding doors at the far end of the bar. 'When there's trouble I close them,' the manager said. 'And shut off the troublemakers from the hotel! Just leave them to themselves!' He told us that on one Easter day 2800 bottles of beer were sold; another day of the Easter holiday they were only allowed to open for two hours, and in that two hours 1100 bottles of beer were sold. 'That's where the money of the hotel is,' he said. 'They'll do anything for beer. That's why I had those doors put in. They go mad! I shut them out and leave them to get on with it. Before the Highlands Highway was built, and the beer came in, they'd never fermented any liquor here.'

Before leaving Mendi we paid a courtesy visit to the newly appointed Papuan District Commissioner, but he had gone to Mount Hagen to meet the Governor-General who was completing his farewell tour by a visit to the Highlands. So we visited the Australian Deputy DC instead. His home was one of a group of pleasant modern houses with gardens set on rising ground. Here we had a drink with three Australians who had been running this savage country. They come of a long line and are instantly recognisable, irrespective of race, these men who are drawn by the challenge of total responsibility in a wild country far from their own. We had been among similar men long ago;

the Frenchmen who administered Morocco before Independence came. Walking up to his house through quiet little suburban gardens, the Queenslander had asked Ralph if he could suggest any sort of job he might try for in Western Australia, which he'd heard we knew well. But what sort of job can you suggest to a man you have seen setting out in the morning with an inclinometer round his neck to survey a new road, and holding a trial for sorcery in the afternoon? A man accustomed to absolute authority, but authority depending only on himself, his own judgement, his own confidence, his own understanding. A man whose very active mind had been occupied throughout most of his adult life with the lives, thoughts, behaviour and problems of people so different from himself, that the effort to understand them was an endless progression of groping and discovery. Men who have introduced the Western concept of impartial justice, and tried to make it understood.

Talking to these men it was difficult to remember this was the 'colony of a colony!' as one of them put it – so closely was the Australian administration based on the English system. Indeed, one senior Australian administrator had said to us, 'I'd rather work for the British than my own people.' And when I asked why, he replied, 'Because the British make very few laws, essential laws, and insist on their being kept. So everyone knows where they are. Other races make too many laws, so they can't be kept, and nobody knows where they are.'

To my surprise they asked us about the Common Market – why should they care? 'Would Britain really stay in?' they asked incredulously. 'Her voice will never be heard among all the Continental powers. England's never done any good on the continent of Europe except for wars and holidays. Her genius has always shown in faraway countries across the sea, and among quite different races.'

Walking down from this house with the *Kiap* from Queensland who had shown us so much, he said, 'I wonder if you'll come to my house for a minute and meet my wife.' I wondered why she hadn't been with us at the Deputy DC's for drinks.

'Maybe she won't want to be invaded,' I said. 'She might not,' he said a trifle grimly and a little later, 'I must warn you she may be in a bad temper!' His house, similar to the one we had just left, was rather untidy, with a Papuan woman working, and two lovely children, a very blonde little girl of about seven and a darker, younger boy. 'I'll fetch my wife,' he said and we heard him go upstairs. He came back without her and we chatted about his future. Probably he would go back to Queensland, 'a cattle station or something', he said. It seemed such a waste of his immense experience. 'I'll see what's happened to her,' he said after a few minutes. He went upstairs again and returned. After a minute she walked in. She was an Aborigine. She stood quite still just inside the door.

When we were in West Australia I'd seen fascinating Aborigine girls in paintings by Elizabeth Durak, painted on her father's vast lands, where they could live and roam much as they had always done. But I had never seen any looking like that in real life; all those I had seen had put on weight from our starchy Western food and lack of exercise, and had become heavy and strangely square. This had happened to her. Had she ever looked like the lissom girls in the Durak pictures? He would have married her in Queensland – when? Not before he came here, judging by the children's ages. On leave from here, then? That very blonde little girl! I'd been told in Australia that in mixed marriages the Aborigine strain died out completely by the second generation, unlike other dark races which survive so long.

I went up to her and apologised for disturbing her and held out my hand. She made no movement, nor did her expression change. I'd never had anyone refuse to shake hands with me before, so I put mine down rather lamely and said something about the children. Ralph came up and – warned – took her hand from her side and shook it and made some conversation. She looked at us passively with opaque, faintly hostile eyes. After a minute she turned and went upstairs again. She had not spoken.

How would it be with them when they were back in Queensland? Would she allow people to make friends with her? Would they try? What else could we have done? He had spent his working life among the mountain Papuans, then had gone back to his own country and married a woman of the only race on earth which is even more remote, primeval, unknowable. What was he seeking?

From Mendi we drove back to Mount Hagen, where we heard law and order had broken down. It was a long drive, hot and dusty and glaring, and always of course the altitude. When we arrived at Mount Hagen Hotel we longed to relax over a bath, a drink, a quiet meal alone. But the manager met us to say two gentlemen were waiting to see us. This modern hotel had large and pleasant lounges, the bedrooms opened off a courtyard. The town still fluttered with the Governor-General's visit yesterday. Apparently much beer had been consumed, hence the breakdown of law and order, as some were fighting drunk.

A tall white man and a short black man got up to greet us in the lounge. A coffee planter who had been in the area twenty years, hearing Ralph was in the Highlands, thought he would be interested to meet Mr Wamp, so brought him along. Mr Wamp must have been over seventy but had the tough, resilient look of a football, and moved with a springy energy. He had the immaculate look that only a very black person in starched white clothes – shirt and shorts – can have. Yesterday he had received the OBE from the Governor-General, representing the Queen. This was in recognition of his services in making available to the white people the land on which the town of Mount Hagen is built. This had been in 1938 when white men first came through, looking for gold. He is the great clan chieftain of the area, an impressive man, very powerful, very rich. He talked the extremely elaborate and complex pidgin English of PNG so fast it was impossible to follow, and the coffee planter translated. Mr Wamp seemed so sophisticated, one felt free to ask him all the unsolved questions in our minds – nothing could possibly shock him. To begin with I was puzzled by his name 'Wamp One' meaning head of the Wamp clan, the top man. Yes, but had he another name? 'No,' he answered brightly. 'I have no Christian name – yet! The missionaries will not accept me because I have not yet finished paying the blood money I owe. This was incurred when I made this land available to the white people to build this town. It is a big area, you see. The land belonged to many people. I hope that when I have paid it all off, the missionaries will accept me, then they will give me a Christian name.' I asked him if the country had any religion of its own, saying I had never before found a country in which there was no form of worship, however vague, however strange, some reaching out to a power beyond the human.

'No,' he said. 'No. There is great belief in spirits, the spirits of the dead. Sometimes it is felt they can help.'

Unlike the Chinese, this is not the idea (which always seems to me very reasonable) that your dead ancestors can be inter-mediaries between you and some higher and immortal spirit. In Papua New Guinea it stops short at the dead person. (The Kiap in Mendi had told us he had seen women wearing a chain of hands and feet round their necks – not of enemies, but of members of their family.)

Mr Wamp enlarged on the possible value of dead ancestors. 'If someone is ill, perhaps a dead relative will be dug up, and the organ eaten which is the organ the sick person is suffering with.'

'And if it doesn't help?'

He shrugged. 'Then they think perhaps they have eaten the wrong piece; after all, any treatment can fail! They would not think it was the method that was wrong. In any case he would be helped because the spirit of his ancestor would have entered into his mind and body.'

He talked quite freely about sorcery, very conscious that with Independence coming his people were between two worlds and would have to look very closely at their old beliefs, which in-cluded sorcery.

He confirmed and amplified all we had learned about the pig and cassowary economy and that 'the more people you have borrowed from, the more people you have interested in your wealth and well-being. At the *Sing-Sing* you display your wealth to clans and people to whom you owe money and say, "Look, this is where it has gone! Look how wealthy I am." Then perhaps you distribute ten per cent of the pigs – you kill them, or sometimes you deliver them alive to people you owe interest to. They take them away but maybe they pass them on to other people, to whom they owe interest. Maybe you have borrowed little pigs, and they become big pigs, so your wealth is increasing all the time.' A very rich man is allowed to wear a sliver of bamboo at the neck, according to the number of people he has borrowed from and these can hang like a necklace or be put sideways to make a pattern. 'A very rich man can wear a necklace of bamboo slivers that reaches almost to the ground.' Mr Wamp was interesting on the problem of modern society upsetting the hierarchy of the clans. Ralph asked him whether leadership of a clan was hereditary. 'Not necessarily,' he said.

'The government of a clan, the elders, is an élite. It tends to stay with the same families, but only if they produce the best people. It will not pass to the eldest son – necessarily – but to one of the sons, the best that can be found. Then the rubbish-men, finding themselves pushed out, may go down to the coast or to Bougainville and come back with a lot of money – new clothes, knowledge – and this is a great problem. So our society is constantly adjusting itself.'

Later that night we talked to the manager after he had locked all the doors and most of the staff had gone home. The few people staying in the hotel were business people, he said, waiting for Independence to see what they could make out of it.

He had run the hotel for about two years, and apparently had very good personal relations in Hagen. He could walk through the town at night which few people did. In case of trouble, he thought that many of his staff would back him up – even when drunk they recognised him and something got through to them. He ran the hotel on a clan basis, members of one clan will run the bar, another act as waiters, another clean the rooms. But fatal to introduce someone, however good, from another clan. They'll do anything to get him out. It's like a union closed shop on a clan basis. They are paid individually, but one man in each clan gets it all, a different one each week; it may be a big sum, a thousand dollars – 'but he may blue it at cards, drink it, bury it, it is his money. He won't get any more till his turn comes round again, perhaps many months later, so he has to borrow.'

In the morning we talked to the head houseboy and he said, 'Yes, they did pool their money, but only the lowest pay. If the head boy got fifteen dollars and the lowest ten, then all he got when it was his turn was his own rate, ten dollars, from each of the others, and they kept the extra.' Papuans seem always to create a complex, interlocking, thin-spreading, far-reaching web of finance, in which no final end is ever reached. The manager expected to be replaced by a local man ultimately, but by then he thought he'd have retired.

University students had been sent up to act as assistant

managers with a view to promotion, but in no time at all money was missing from the till, bottles were missing – trouble everywhere; they were squeezed out by sheer pressure of the staff, combining to get rid of the outsiders.

Meantime Mr Wamp had gone home. His village was about three miles out of Mount Hagen. He had told us about his family. He had six wives and had had twenty-six children. Three girls and three boys had died, so he now had twenty children – 'Very expensive!' he said. When at home he lived in a village house – a *kunai* – and his wives lived in the women's house. At home he dressed like the rest of his clan; not our Mr Wamp with the Queen's ribbon on his sparkling white shirt; but Wamp One, the chief of his clan, in a spray of leaves and a fold of cloth – and, I suspect, many many bamboo slivers. A man of two worlds – very well balanced between them, it seemed.

But I think the hospital at Mendi had shown the sharpest confrontation. It was the most pleasant hospital I ever saw, the group of huts in open grassland. A clear demonstration of Albert Schweitzer's vision in starting, long ago in Africa, an 'open' hospital. It casts out fear. We had seen so many hospitals in other countries that people wouldn't go to until it was too late, if then, and it is easy to understand how they feared offering themselves up to an alien building which might have been a prison once the doors shut behind them – cut off from their families for an unknown time, anything might be done to them. But in this building all the doors were open, and the walls seemed to be chiefly windows. The patients' families came with them and camped outside on the grass – they brought their dogs, who wandered in occasionally and were not too seriously shooed out. So they could receive treatment, and their families, should any need help in the future, would know what it was like and would come without fear. A man's ward, a woman's ward; a little boy slung in a kind of hammock, he was terribly burned, having rolled into the fire.

The nurses were Australian, New Zealanders, and one English girl from Birmingham who was working her way round the world as a nurse. Her last job had been in Canada. When the

Kiap introduced us, there was a vague little laugh, which I didn't quite understand. After he'd shown us round and we were leaving, the senior nurse came forward and said, 'We realise it's true – you are Hammond Innes – a legend come to life. We thought it was a joke, just someone who looked like you. Would you like a cup of tea?' The *Kiap* went off to see someone, and we sat round a table with the nurses and had tea. I suppose it was their sitting-room, but everything seemed so open you could see through to the wards. The nurses were all young. Their hospital had an air of meticulous organisation, for all the deliberate surface informality. One felt everything was under control and that people would get well here if that were possible. Our questions started a conversation among themselves. 'I sometimes wonder what we're doing here,' the girl from Birmingham said. 'We do some good medically, but what the balance is against the illnesses we've imported, would make an interesting debate. By and large I'd say their physical condition compares favourably with ours. And they certainly don't need mental homes which absorb such a large part of our population! They suffer from malnutrition by our standards (their deficiency isn't protein by the way, it's carbohydrates). But then the West is grossly overfed, clogged with food. Look at the distances these people walk! Not from necessity – they go because they want to.'

'Among the illnesses we've imported I'd include beer,' another girl said. 'All the bad injuries we get in here are after they've been into town and got beer. There have always been killings, but that's a personal matter – person against person, individual feuds. Not general mayhem for no reason.'

'Bit of trouble back home when they've been on the beer,' another Australian girl said.

'Yes, but it's different. Some people stick a knife into living flesh more happily than others.'

'What'll happen when Independence comes?' Ralph asked.

'God knows. It won't affect the Highlands much at first. Everything will seep gradually from the towns.'

'They're planning a big new airport – more roads, more

hotels. Trying to launch the Highlands as a tourist resort.' There
was a little laugh.

'They tried a bit of that a few years ago, but nobody much
came.'

'The people take to our things very quickly, but use them
differently. They learned our money quickly – and look at the
plastics they take home.'

'A jerrican's more prestige than a skin for carrying water, but
it's much more awkward to carry.'

'You can't put the clock back,' someone murmured, and that
cliché killed the conversation.

'What do you think?' I asked the Birmingham girl. She
seemed the most thoughtful and concerned, perhaps because she
had seen more of the world.

'Me?' She glanced out to the patients, so black in their white
beds, and beyond to their families camped on the rough grass
with their children and dogs and cooking pots and full *bilum*
bags. And beyond to the hazy mountains from which they came.
Then she turned back and put her white elbows on the scrubbed
table and said, 'I think it would be better if we'd never come.'

Part III

PAKISTAN

Land of Ghosts and Plastic

BANKS OF VIOLETS and stinking drains. The Great Trunk Road much as Kipling described it, except for the added complication of motor traffic. Particularly the painted buses – buses covered with pictures. When you buy a new bus, I discovered, you take it to an artist who specialises in this work, and have it painted all over with coloured pictures, as mixed as a scrapbook. Of course, the number and detail depend on how much you can pay, but at their best they are very ambitious; faces, flowers, monsters, landscapes, buildings, decorative patterns, using every colour in the world, each picture contained in a neat rectangle. These decorated buses stand out in open country, weaving through the flat green Indus plain, or climbing the bare and barren rocks leading to the Khyber Pass. Massed in the cities they are as brilliant as a flower market. It goes without saying that they are full; this doesn't just mean that the seats are occupied – (has anyone ever seen an empty seat? Are there seats?). They are submerged. Bodies bulge out of doors and windows, the roof, the back, every available inch. This crowding, this movement, the need to fill every surface with decoration; these buses express much of Pakistan.

But the Great Trunk Road, slashed across the country from Calcutta to Kabul, is still Kim's. The heaviest loads, timber and concrete, are drawn by slow-moving buffaloes, massive, imperturbable, black. The smallest are the little water carts, always drawn by the tiniest splay-legged ponies and driven by the shabbiest old men. In between are the briskly trotting *tonga* ponies, overloaded to a point that shocks credulity; I have counted twenty people packed and piled on to one of these small two-wheeled carts. Smart cars arrogantly hooting, battered cars, taxis, donkey carts; the pace of the road is fast, moving round the slow-moving ox carts. How can they all find space for themselves? I suppose the ones who couldn't are dead. I first saw the Great Trunk Road after heavy floods, driving north from Rawalpindi. Herds of buffalo had been brought up from the waterlogged lower land to stand at the side of the road between the garages, blacksmiths' forges, shops, cafés; with here and there someone wrapped in a cloak asleep, here and there a man being shaved.

We had entered Pakistan at Karachi. Apart from travellers, and people meeting them, one was faced at the airport by a tight-packed crowd of spectators. I remembered my mother, who had come to India as a missionary, then after her marriage, moved into a different kind of life, saying, 'In India there's always a crowd, they rise up out of the ground.' A burly man with a strong, rather quizzical face pushed through to us with an air of authority and held out his hand. 'I am Rahim,' he said, with a smile of great warmth and charm. This was a Pathan general we had been put in touch with by an English friend, an Air Marshal; they had met on a senior officers' course at the end of the war, and their friendship had lasted.

Driving us from the airport he was much too courteous to express surprise at our choice of hotel. Ralph always rejects tourist hotels, as their object is to insulate you from the country – which in our case is what we have come to discover. So we go to local hotels, not international hotels, if that is at all possible. But as another Indian friend was to say to us later, 'Sometimes that might be a little unwise.'

Our large room looked over a courtyard as big as a town square. Usually this was hidden by a tarpaulin, but after torrential rain had filled it (not the monsoon, but 'unscheduled rain') it was taken down. Across the courtyard, open-fronted rooms on the ground floor made a stage set for children dancing – rehearsing for something? They wove in slow patterns, moved chairs, sat down on the floor to talk, then rose to weave again. Every night there were parties on the edge of the courtyard, with much passing to and fro of servants carrying trays and dishes. Above, four floors of bedrooms housed their secrets, sometimes a figure hurried along the balconies on an unknown errand. To our right was a long ornamental pool, and after the rain men sat all day on the edge fishing out twigs and leaves, while others swabbed up the water from the terrace into buckets – slowly, going on all day. Above them in tall trees the kites were nesting; we watched one pair build their nest, and before we left she was sitting on her eggs. Always kites hung in the sky.

It was as well to look out of the window, as the room was depressing. Each day I wrote another letter of my name in the dust on the dark brown furniture. Yards of trailing flex looped on to nails led to lights that didn't work. In the bathroom we traced the flood on the stone floor to seepage under the wall from the next bathroom. The lavatory didn't flush during certain hours, as the water was turned off, not to conserve water but to rest the plumbing. Complaints produced a crowd of men who occupied the place with much chatter but failed to get results; but at least we did get the wall plastered up between our bathroom and the next. I gradually came to feel that the word plumbing does not conjugate with the word Pakistan. In private houses of great luxury and beauty the bathrooms can be incongruously rough, and even when charmingly appointed, there will be a basin not quite fixed to the wall, and spasmodic flushing. One feels the country doubts the whole principle of piped water being under control. It's an idea the English introduced, and it doesn't seem to have progressed since they left. The most interesting bathrooms are the ones with an open bricked gully for the bathwater to flow out, exactly the same as the one where Rikki Tikki Tavi watched for the cobras.

Fortunately we weren't in much. The Rahims gave a splendid dinner party for us the night we arrived, and from then on we had a dinner party or reception every night we were in the country. We had arrived with introductions to a few people in each of the five cities, and as this is a feudal country, they fanned out endlessly. So we were plunged into an exotic world, suddenly a part of it, looking out through other eyes, from inside other homes, other families. I had not been prepared for the charm of the people – these enchanting women! So decorative, in their soft vivid clothes, saris, or baggy trousers and long fitted tunic, with a scarf thrown over back-to-front. The Prophet had decreed a woman should be covered from her neck to her ankles. I wonder if he foresaw how seductive the result would be? But also their personalities are so warm and lively; at every party I met women I felt could have become friends. Many of the men had been to Sandhurst, Oxford or the Inns of Court, according to their calling, and so their manner was deceptively home-like. Deceptively? Could centuries of different experience, behaviour, values, be lost under a few Western years?

Two days before we arrived, President Zia had announced his new 'austerity' laws, of which the most immediately noticeable was the banning of alcohol. This meant that for about two hours one talked to a succession of strangers on the strength of fresh orange or tomato juice. Our hosts, everywhere, insisted on fetching us. Courtesy? Caution? So smoothly was the social life conducted one almost forgot the country was under martial law, and that Bhutto, recently President, was in prison under sentence of death. But this country had never known peace or security. Artificially created by Partition from the rest of India in 1947, this rending apart threw up the most violent chaos of refugees the world had ever seen (or so it was said at the time). In the thirty years since then, they had fought two wars with India, winning the first and losing the second – not to the

Indians but to the Americans, they said, because the USA
stopped supplying them with arms, whereas Russia continued to supply India. Then the bitter, inconclusive war with
their other-half, Eastern Pakistan, which broke off and became
Bangladesh. Endless changes of government, many periods
of military dictatorship; I think they were used to maintaining
their way of life on a thin crust over chaos. 'The lid is still
held down on the pot, but the pot is boiling,' someone said to
us.

At our first parties in Karachi I had a bad cold, something
I hardly ever have, caught on the plane, I suppose, and a cough
which made a man I sat next to at dinner say with almost awed
sympathy, 'My dear! – That's a real churchyard!' Struggling
with these awkward shames, and badly needing a drink
(alcoholic), I still enjoyed these evenings; conversation after
conversation, person after person, the big room full of dark and
different faces. Not before ten o'clock were the doors thrown
open into the dining-room, and we saw the glory of the table,
decorated with strange flowers and fruits, covered with an infinite variety of spicy dishes. And later, the blancmange-like
puddings in pretty colours, decorated with silverleaf (I didn't
realise at first that this was edible, and used to scrape it off). And
always the bowl of yoghourt, taken as a very necessary digestive.
Shortly after dinner, people began to go home.

These, with variations of greater and lesser houses, set the
pattern for almost all our evenings. We seemed borne along
on a wave of colour and talk, a perpetual quiver of animation.

Rahim drove us without comment the length of an unfinished
and abandoned building site along the shore. Away to our right,
across grey sand and sea, a long queue of ships waited their turn
to get into the port of Karachi. On our left a seemingly endless
line of tall grey unfinished houses standing in rubble stared with
empty window-spaces at the sea. They became more and more
despairingly abandoned as one drove, and still the line of
unfinished houses stretched along the desolate shore. Once or
twice a few men with a small pony and cart were bringing sand
from the beach across the road to make bricks; it seemed a puny

effort. I don't think we ever did get to the end of that grandiose housing project which had come to grief.

Returning past this desolation, we came upon a congested caravanserai of tents; men, mules and horses, everything dusty and desert brown, crowded and animated, everyone moving about and shouting to each other. This was a transit camp for people who had brought country wares into the city. Then the road wound up a hill through trees, and high above it all, screened in the mercy of green, we visited Rahim's eldest daughter in her married home. She came like a fairy princess in her gossamer clothes through her big white drawing-room full of beautiful things to greet us. A servant brought soft drinks and toasted pine kernels. Her little son ran in followed by his *ayah*. Rahim withdrew unobtrusively into the terraced garden full of moist greenery and brilliant flowers to say his prayers (as Moslems do at certain times during the day). The windows framed the sunset, colouring a wide distant view.

In Karachi I saw my first bazaar. One of my new friends with the glamorous name of Yasmina said, 'I am going to choose a carpet as a wedding present for a friend's daughter, would you like to come?'

How she drove her car through those streets and found somewhere to leave it, I shall never know; narrow seething streets with small open shops on either side. I suppose you just push gently and things give way. At the corner where we stopped was a sugar-cane stall – you suck the long brown bars. A man passed swinging a figure-of-eight-shaped cage of stiff green netting in which a newly caught batch of small green parrots clambered and clawed endlessly. The clop of ponies' feet and the hooting of motor horns stood out from the miasma of voices. Slowly, implacably, the river of people and animals and vehicles and merchandise surges on.

The shops look small from the front but they go back a long way and are stacked with goods. Yasmina sat in her favourite carpet shop and they laid rugs before her. She asked them to show me, just for interest, something very special which a millionaire friend of her husband's had bought to take back to

Switzerland with him; very small, very old, a silk picture of Adam and Eve. He would hang it on a wall and look at it, look into it, as long as at a fine painting. I forget how many thousands he had paid for it.

Then she took me to a shop selling fabrics, and I made my first purchase in the country as a souvenir of my first bazaar; two lengths of material in the same print, one silky, one gossamer.

Meantime Ralph, with his usual prescience of what place would become significant, was agitating to get along the coast of Baluchistan to Gwadar and beyond that, if possible to Jiwani. They were fishing ports on the coast, very close to the Iranian frontier. They could be developed to command the Gulf, failing possession of Karachi.

Driving north from Karachi we had seen the Russian steel factory ('The Americans wouldn't give it to us, and we had to get it from somewhere') and on the opposite side of the road the barracks for their work people; 'little Russia' our friends called it. The Russians had started a Goodwill Club to entertain the local people, with the result that already you heard Russian being spoken in the bazaars.

Baluchistan was a no-go area. You had to apply to the Home Secretary for a pass, which was always refused. Perhaps he just liked to know who wanted one? A friend of ours, lunching with a friend of his who was concerned with Baluchistan, said, 'I don't think there's any reason why the Hammond Inneses shouldn't go to Gwadar, do you?' And his friend answered, 'No. Now what would be the best way of arranging that? I think the best thing is that they should go as the personal guests of the officer commanding the Coastguards there.'

So we flew along that pale coast, looking inland to the arid mountains, and came down on to sand, the landing strip being on the shore beside the fishing village. Here it was blazing hot and glaring. Ralph had his camera out, and walked towards the group of people watching – the plane being the only contact with the outside world. A guard with a gun tapped him on the shoulder and shook his head. Ralph nodded and put his camera away, smiling; no point in trying to explain he only wanted to photograph the faces, not the place.

The adjutant of the Coastguards had come to meet us. The Coastguards were a civil organisation but were officered by the Army. He swept us into a military car and we drove away down an avenue of trees. Otherwise, we should have been sent back on the same plane. We were taken to the guest bungalow, at the end of a line of bungalows between the desert and the shore. Two camp beds, their army blankets neatly folded, in the middle of the room; a table, two chairs, cupboards against the wall for our possessions. A large bare stone bathroom, with the usual stream of water across the floor, but with wooden slats to stand on like islands, so you could kick your sandals off at the door and make your way as on stepping stones from shower to wash basin to lavatory. This hospitality for strange guests in a remote place was surprising and enjoyable. I liked waking to the sound of the *muezzin* every morning.

As often happens to me, I didn't realise until I thought about it later just how extraordinary my position was; a Western woman as the guest of a Muslim officers' mess, in a sensitive area of a wild country. At the time, I am always too busy trying to adapt.

We unpacked, then went for a walk along the shore to see the sun go down. Strange fishing boats drawn up, a little boy bicycling along the hard sand, two dogs excavating something in a sandhill. A jeep came along, and a very well-dressed gentleman got out and greeted us warmly. He introduced himself as the Assistant District Commissioner. He hoped we would enjoy our visit. We wrung each other's hands, assured him we didn't want a lift, and he passed on. We continued our walk. The sun reddened as it dropped towards the sea, and the water took on the oily look of evening.

Another vehicle came along and also stopped beside us. This gentleman also greeted us with the utmost friendliness and welcomed us. He was the Customs Officer, he said. He drove on and we chose a certain rock to be the furthest point of our walk, from there we would turn back. The sun would disappear in a minute and the dark would come quickly ... Shortly after we turned a third vehicle came into sight, also with one man in it, driving along the sand. 'So much traffic,' Ralph said. 'Do they always do this? Will he stop too?' Yes, and greeted us. 'I am the Agronomist,' he said. (A pleasant cover for Intelligence, where the usual euphemism of Passport Officer would not apply?)

'It's usual for desert people to greet strangers,' Ralph remarked as the Agronomist drove away, 'and to offer us lifts in a country where few people walk if they don't have to. Just odd that such an improbable trio should all be driving along the sands within half an hour of each other.'

I walked along the verandah to the mess for dinner the first evening with slight trepidation, though it's odd how much one takes things for granted when they're actually happening – a dreamlike acceptance of the improbable. They all stood up when we went in. If they hadn't been to Sandhurst they took their behaviour from others who had – and their shirts. There were five, all dark, tall and handsome, in fact I found it difficult at first to tell them apart and remember names and ranks. They were all young, in immaculate light khaki.

Soft drinks, of course, under President Zia's new orders. I asked for a Coke and they brought me one, which I learned too late was their last (supplies hadn't been trucked in because the desert was under flood). I sat on the Colonel's right, Ralph opposite me. The Colonel was slightly older than the others, and had travelled in Europe. He could take the English 'boiled food' but had been sick in Paris. We had soup, meat with the usual peppery spices, rice, one of the soft blancmangey puddings. Looking round the table, I was conscious that these men were descended from endless generations to whom fighting was the natural – inevitable – way of life. I had heard that, given comparable arms, they were probably the most formidable fighting men in the world. There was a certain piquancy in contrasting the English-style manner and dress, and a naivety about our world, with what they would be – had been – in action, functioning in their own world, the thing they understood.

Conversation was no more difficult to maintain than in many groups who have more in common.

A brief ritual terminated every meal, toothpick drill. Each officer took one from the table and set about using it with total concentration, the left hand cupped neatly over the busy right hand. Silence fell upon the table. I had never known this practice treated so seriously. Could it, I wondered, relate to the older custom of cleaning the teeth with a root or twig? I know that many parts of the world regard our toothbrush as a disgustingly unhygienic method.

But it was after dinner every evening, when one or two would linger and we relaxed into armchairs at the other end of the room, that conversation became more challenging. One of them had visited the USA to visit his brother who was a practising psychologist there. 'Very successful. But I am very anxious about him. He is treating these people, but he is becoming infected – he is becoming as bad as they are! He worries, like an American. What is wrong with the Americans, mentally, that they always worry? I do not understand it. I am a Muslim, so are all my family of course. Now, another brother, my youngest, he has just failed an exam. But he doesn't worry. He says to himself, "It is not the will of Allah I should pass the exam this time." If he were an American boy he would be worrying himself sick. I used to discuss with my brother in America far into the night. I don't think he realised how far he had slipped.'

Another evening, another enquiring mind. 'What about the Christian religion? Is there still much of it?' Ralph stretched out in the long chair and said, 'Well now, there are the Wee Frees.' I suspected he would embark on a detailed account of the peculiarities he had discovered in a small island off the west coast of Scotland when he'd been researching for *Atlantic Fury*, and I feared the impression made would be as odd as if the human body were to be explained in terms of the little toe. I felt he was opting out, and I thought we should do better.

'The Christian religion divides into two main groups, Protestant and Catholic,' I began, striving for bold outlines.

'The Catholic Church is much richer. The Vatican, where the Pope rules, has vast wealth ...'

'Wealth?' he interrupted with a gently pitying smile of disbelief. 'Oh no! No! ...'

It had been a long day in the heat. The Colonel had driven us along the cliffs where the monsoon wind could blow so strongly that people and vehicles were blown over to the beach below. But a relentlessly dry wind, the monsoon having spent all its moisture before reaching here – hence the strangeness of the recent unseasonal floods. This was the coast where Alexander's army had finally disintegrated, their furthest point from home. Many died, some tried to make the endless journey home, many just stopped, and merged into the life of the people, and left a Greek strain in the race.

A look-out hut on the cliff was still intact. 'The British built it. They build well.' Strange shells lie about, flung up by abnormal waves; there is nothing to bury them in this place that never knows rain. Further along the coast, he drove us up many hairpin bends to a breathtakingly unexpected oasis; very high, cradled in the rocks, dazzling green; a little lake with graceful trees and bright flowers. He helped me scramble over the rocks, then produced a Thermos of coffee out of his car, and we drank it in cool shade.

Back on ground level, he showed us a very modern solar distillation plant with rows of open tanks through which the water filtered. This was a pilot scheme, primarily for the military, but if successful, it would revolutionise the life of the village, and of other parched villages.

On the way back, the Colonel wished to visit the Assistant District Commissioner at his office. In the town – a row of little shops above the beach – we visited the first gentleman who had inspected us the night of our arrival.

'Ah!' the Colonel said expansively, 'he is Lord of the Day!'

'What do you mean?' Ralph asked.

'I mean he is Lord of the Day! He is ruler. If he says "Off with his head" then that man's head falls.'

The Lord of the Day smiled agreeably and offered us coffee.

I took the phrase as a joke, but wondered why the Colonel, a very sensible and responsible man, wished to establish the point so strongly. I think he probably wanted to protect his good relations with the civil authority by taking us to see the ADC, and impressing upon us how important he was, so he should not feel affronted by the military having foreign civilian visitors in a no-go area.

After coffee, and admiring the excellent maps on the office walls, the Colonel went back to the mess, and we said we would explore the town. Coming out of a cigarette shop, a car stopped beside us and who should greet us but the Customs Officer. It seemed inevitable that a few minutes later, at the end of the street, we should meet the Agronomist.

The Colonel lent us a Land Rover and his best driver to take us to Jiwani, our second objective. We drove north towards the Iranian border. When the track ended we struck out across the desert, after a couple of hours our way was blocked by large areas of flood, rare to the point of being unprecedented. We saw one painted truck bogged down. We came to a small sea, too big to go round, so the driver charged it. Ralph was watching the driving. Looking down, I saw the water had risen to his knees through the floor of the Land Rover. I called to him to pull his feet up, as I had snatched mine. We got through that, and several minor ones. From time to time we saw camels in the distance, otherwise nothing till the apparent towers of a great ruined city grew out of the distance. But it was the rock formation along the shore. You could have sworn it was buildings – castles, houses, spires, fortifications.

At Jiwani on the Iranian border, we looked across Iran to the Gulf of Hormuz. Only one young officer occupied the Mess. He gave us lunch. Like so many of them, he had been a prisoner during the second Indian war for many months, looking out over the Fort at Delhi from his cell. 'Conditions very bad.' He, too, took us along the cliffs, and on a high point the remains of a British barracks, in excellent repair on that desolate wind-swept headland. 'Still good!' he said. 'It could be used again. Perhaps will be!' We wandered through the rooms, reading the

English names scratched on the walls by men bored with looking out over that empty sea, dreaming of home and green grass.

We also wandered through a small deserted palace, ornately planned, briefly occupied, then abandoned, a few flowers still struggling through the sand in the crumbling courtyards. From here no one had looked out, the high walls enclosed you, interest was within.

And who should we meet in Jiwani but our three wise men, the ADC, the Customs Officer, and the Agronomist, who 'just happened to have business there!' How had they got there? Why? To take all that trouble ...

On the return journey, to avoid some of the floods, we drove for miles along the seashore, the waves on our right, and on our left the incredible white rock formation; a towering, always changing decoration carved in ivory, sometimes flushed with flesh-colour.

When we got home, I stood outside on the verandah and shook my clothes and beat my shoes to get rid of the worst of the sand before entering our room, but my eyelashes and eyebrows and hair were stiff and white with sand.

The Adjutant's wife was visiting him, but she kept strict purdah and remained in their bungalow. She came tripping along the verandah to talk to me – as much as two women can talk who have no word of common language! Fortunately she brought her little boy with her, and one can always talk at or around a child. She was young and pretty, I was interested in her make-up; nails painted on hands and feet, eye make-up and lipstick; a dainty sari, lots of bangles.

On our last night, they gave a dinner party for us. I had heard the roar of voices as I changed, and servants hurrying to and fro; the chairs had been borrowed from our room. I am used to being the only woman in a group, but I felt a little trepidatious as I stood outside the mess door.

The room was very full. Everyone stopped talking and stood up. In addition to the full Mess, there were some distinguished military visitors, and a number of local dignitaries. The Colonel introduced us to everyone punctiliously. Of course our old friends the ADC, the Customs Officer, and the Agronomist were there. Also the District Commissioner, a short stout man with a beard who talked continuously. Then fortunately, there was so much noise and animation in the room that we could merge into it.

The morning we left, we realised our visit had set them some problems. The Colonel, a man of great charm and authority, had made it all seem easy and natural. But when Ralph was asked to take our passports to the office, he was gone a long time. Over endless cups of coffee, endless telephone conversations took place in Urdu. I don't think we had bothered them personally – I think they meant it when they said that to a unit completely cut off, it was a pleasure to have people from the outside world to talk to, and the atmosphere had been so relaxed and friendly. But the moment came when forms had to be filled in that would satisfy the bureaucratic filing system, and they didn't quite know how to explain us. (The Colonel had said goodbye early, as he was accompanying one of last night's guests to his post in the North.)

When we flew back to Karachi the great heat had struck. This time we stayed with the Rahims in great delight. Imtiaz, Rahim's wife, had arranged a dinner party for us that night, and without an apparent glance at my sand- and sweat-soaked head, sweetly anticipated my need; 'If Dorothy would like to have her hair done, I will take her to my hairdresser.'

He was very good. He asked if I had my hair done by a man or a woman in London, and went on, 'If he should like a Pakistan assistant, I would come. I can do everything – perms, colour, cutting. If I had a job to come to, I could get a permit, you see.' One sensed the desperate urgency to get out, to a country where the pressures were less. His hairdryer was hard to start, it had been repaired so often. He explained the impossibility of getting new equipment. He could only get new brushes through 'a friend who has a special arrangement'. 'Very expensive, as I must pay him, as well as for the brushes.'

At the party, we met one of Imtiaz's friends who, with her, had mounted an exhibition of Pakistan crafts in Texas the year before. I could imagine how these energetic Indian ladies in their lovely saris would have wowed the Texans. We had seen Imtiaz in action once (at the airport, on our behalf) – sweeping all before her with smiling charm and determination, a light in her eyes as of one playing a game she enjoyed, and knew she could win. They had meant to have an exhibition in Iran the following year '. . . but not now.' Some of our new friends who had relations in Iran were desperately on the telephone to know if they were safe, when they could come home.

One of Rahim and Imtiaz's daughters was training to be a nurse, and working part-time at the hospital. She confirmed sadly what we had heard, that though the doctors were good, there was a great shortage of nurses, and it was impossible to get responsible ward-servants as it is unusual for women to go out to work; that cats had been brought in to keep down the rats, and had become so big and bold they invaded the wards, and had even taken newborn babies from their sleeping mothers' arms. In this country the savage always brushes the exquisite.

When we flew on to Rawalpindi, we were surprised but glad to find a fire lit in our pleasant sitting-room at Flashmans. This famous old hotel was named after its original owner, when it had started life as a private house. Greatly enlarged and modernised, its bungalow units cover a considerable area. Indian servants hurried along the flowery paths carrying covered trays of food. The old man who looked after our room was immensely proud to have served under the British, and indeed, someone had trained him well. But I was always fascinated by the gap between the meticulous care with which familiar routines were executed (every knife and fork exactly so) and the blindness over anything unexpected (clearing away last night's orange peel, or supplying a missing pillowcase). The Bhutto trial was in its final stages nearby, and we sometimes passed in the pathways of Flashmans a strapping blonde English girl who looked at us curiously (Western people generally stayed at the Inter-continental Hotel, a well-insulated island which we found rather alien). We were told she was an old friend of Bhutto's daughter from their Oxford student days, and that she was the chief contact between the Bhutto family and the Western press. Driving home after dining with the Bhandara family, owners of the legendary Murree Brewery, we passed the prison, a long low white house with flowers trained over it, looking more attractive than either the official residence or Bhutto's own house, both now standing empty. Is it a façade? Two armed guards stepped forward and stopped the car, recognised Minoo Bhandara who was driving us, and waved us on.

Sometimes we went across from Flashmans to lunch at a restaurant which an English food commentator had praised – presumably in a mood of mordant humour. In the gutter outside lived one of the wraith-like dogs I had seen in several places. A degree of starvation where the animal appears almost transparent. A large-boned white dog, with the lines of an English Setter, seemed particularly prone to reach this stage. Bowed almost to a hoop, still with the ghost of a beautiful feathered coat, they move endlessly searching for some scrap. And the high-pitched babble when they are kicked, surely those bones must crack.

And we saw the Hanging Gardens, still winter bare, with the banks of inset lights over which the water pours on summer nights. I had never understood about 'hanging' gardens, but looking up from the bottom of all the steps, one saw each level layered as if in space. Two men came with a caged bird, hung the cage in a tree where there were free birds, and sat down on a seat for a little while, then covered up the cage and went off. Was this its treat? And if so, was it the pleasure or tantalus?

We became familiar with the drive out to Islamabad, where all the Embassies are, and many charming private houses. Another administrative city, like Washington and Canberra, serenely isolated from the rest of the country. Here – except that she was everywhere! – lived Vicki Noon, fascinating coppery-haired widow of Feroz Khan Noon, who had been Prime Minister in 1957–58. She had been given ministerial rank to organise tourism in Pakistan – a daunting job even before Zia banned alcohol, but she was attacking it with magnificent energy and initiative. She drove us north to Abbotabad for our first breath of the mountains, and opened her house there for a picnic lunch, and in her garden I first saw the banks of long-stemmed violets, big, gloriously scented. Abbotabad had been cut off by snow till a few days before, and the steep villages we drove through still had drifts beside the road.

The *Pakistan Times*, the largest circulation English language newspaper in the country, was delivered with our breakfast in almost every city, and I read it regularly, struggling with dim light. It is, of course, written by and for English-speaking Indians, as there are very, very few English in the country. It's a good paper, I thought, though it reflected a tendency to assume that if a problem had been defined, and a solution suggested, then that problem was already solved. 'Blindness to be Cured', a headline told me. Underneath I read that a committee had suggested an organisation should be formed to inspect eyes. A letter headed 'Zoo Matters' caught my eye in the Correspondence Column one day. A Mr Kamran Shafi, of Lahore, wrote: 'I visited the Lahore Zoo some days ago and was appalled at the living conditions of the wretched animals.' He listed four points, finishing, 'When man enslaves animals it is his bounden duty to make them as comfortable as possible.' A few days later there was a follow-up – another Lahore gentleman, also writing a thoughtful, good letter, saying one fault was in the Administrator of the Zoo being a vet, who thought his duty ended with the animals' physical condition, and had no knowledge of their psychological needs.

Another day there was a charming letter headed, *Ladies Offended*. 'Ours is an Islamic country. Then may I ask our Pakistan men where they were when an unknown man slapped a young woman in a confectionery shop? Did those *goondas* have the right to accost women unknown to them on the road with such vulgarity? Sir, through your esteemed paper I would like to appeal to the authorities on behalf of myself and other non-purdah-observing women for the protection of our rights. It is a pity that the world over women are demanding their rights – whereas we Muslim women who have from time immemorial been given our rights are afraid that they are going to be snatched away again due to some "rotten elements" in the society who do not know what the word respect means.'

An endless correspondence continued throughout my reading of the *Pakistan Times* in every city about 'Keeping our English Language pure' not defiled by American slang.

Again PIA, that excellent flying bus service, took us on to Lahore. A haunted name. As Angus Wilson says, 'In Lahore City, it seems, there could be nothing more to write, for it has all been said by Kipling.' This is where, 'in the heavy wet heat of an August night', unable to sleep, Kipling walked and walked; his City of Dreadful Night, and Angus Wilson mentions 'that sense of menace, of falling apart'.

But driving from the airport into the city, one's first impression is of wide streets and many trees. In the middle of the road, opposite the Museum of which Kipling's father was Curator, stands the famous gun Zam Zammah – famous because a ragged urchin who never lived was imagined to have sat astride it, delightedly yelling down rudenesses to anyone who would listen. How the great characters of fiction become as real as historical characters! Nothing will ever dislodge Kim from Zam Zammah.

A great fort; a great Mosque, with soldiers on guard day and night round the tomb of the poet Iqbal, so greatly is he honoured. We met his son, a High Court Judge, with a very beautiful wife whose saris were particularly glorious, and a lovely house full of treasures.

Remembering the letters in the *Pakistan Times*, I felt that as a matter of conscience we should visit the Zoo. The cages of the big animals were in a circular block which you could walk right round – panthers, lions, tigers. A wolf. Having got one's eye in to the North American Timber wolf (through films), this Indian wolf looked small. He came on light, dainty, hesitant feet to the bars of his cage and poised on his toes, looking at us with pale searching eyes. But these were Mowgli's wolves; this was Grey Brother. He had been caught quite near here, they said. I asked how long he had been there. About ten years, they said. *Alone.*

These social animals with their close family life and their wide roaming. In that small concrete cell.

A cage of tigers. The Superintendent of the Zoo ran up to their cage waving his arms and whooping them up like a circus master to stir them into action, and they slowly rose a little, snarling. They had been supplied by London Zoo, we were told. Is such irony possible? That they should be sent back like so much merchandise to the continent from which they or their parents must have come, to live in prison here?

Then they showed us their prize exhibit. 'We have a Snow Leopard! A young one, we haven't had him long. Very rare!' His cage was the end one. 'Air conditioned!' they said proudly. At first I thought the cage was empty. Then in the back right-hand corner I saw a line of beautiful fur. He was lying with his face to the wall on a concrete shelf above the ground, stretched out quite motionless. 'Shall we stir him up? So you can see him?' 'No,' we said. 'No, leave him.' How would he look when he turned – still wondering if this might be release? Or had he already despaired? How could we meet his eyes, standing outside his cage among his captors. Let him keep whatever half-escape into dozing he had found. Very long, thick fur, white speckled with dark.

We went sickly away. Our driver, who had accompanied us, broke the silence. 'Perhaps it is not good,' he said thoughtfully as he drove us away. Then after a minute he said, 'Our prisons are not good, either. It is not only the zoos that are over-crowded.'

A charming Parsee friend asked, 'Have you seen everything in Lahore that you want to?' and I told him we had not seen the Old City, which I particularly wanted to see, because we'd been told that after the heavy rains the mud streets would be difficult to drive.

'They have been, but it's better now, we'll take you. I know! We'll go at night and see the Red Light district. I will arrange it with the owner of the cinema there. He is very powerful, very rich. He will arrange that we see the best dancers. The dancers

133

of Lahore are very special, very famous, they are the finest you will ever see.'

Judge Iqbal's beautiful wife said she would like to come with us. 'All right,' he said, 'You may go. I will mention to the chief of police, this little expedition.'

We met at ten o'clock the following night. The Gate to the Old City had been pointed out to me before, but in the mystery of darkness I could not relate it to the other parts of Lahore which I knew. We drove along the central street of the Red Light District. The pale houses on either side were tall, four-storeys. In most of them, windows on every floor were open and the rooms brightly lit, with several girls sitting in a row in each window. Their make-up was very white (light skins are admired), with eyes and lips heavily painted, so they looked like dollies. They were young, some of them talking and laughing among themselves, but without turning their faces from the front. In a few rooms, an animated little tea party was taking place, entertaining callers. In a few rooms, the shutters were already closed.

The street was thronged with people – a few *tongas*, a few cars. Cows were settling down for the night, lying against the wall of the houses to sleep on the muddy ground. High, high between the houses and their balconies you could see the sky. It was a very long street, closing in the hubbub of voices. We reached a quiet little square at the end of the street. Here was the cinema, and our host went in to find the manager. Through open windows we watched an Indian film; long conversations between elaborately dressed characters, making faces and gestures of melodramatic despair.

Our host came back with the manager and his bodyguards. He was the boss of this place, I gathered. We were introduced, and he kindly said he would escort us himself. He was wearing a dark, well-cut western suit, and he had the sort of figure, slim and waisted, that somehow suggested steel corsets. His bodyguards fell in, one on either side of him. Burly and alert and silent, they looked capable of guarding anyone from anything.

The three of them went first, our little party followed. We

were six, our Parsee host and hostess, the beautiful wife of the judge, pulling her sari across her face as she glanced around her with interest, an Englishman who was staying with our host, Ralph and myself. We followed the three, the dark slim central figure and the burly men on either side who never looked ahead, but always to left and right.

'He wants us to see two dancers, they're expecting us,' our host said as we tried to keep together through the moving crowd. I don't know when during the evening I had my pocket picked – only a scarf and a little loose change, silly of me to have them there. It is only worth mentioning because I was wearing a fitted coat with flat deep pockets, I could hardly get my own hand down without unbuttoning the coat, yet I felt nothing at all. Ralph whispered to me, 'This is possibly the most dangerous place we've ever been in.' I was surprised, I don't know why he said it, why he felt it; nothing you could take hold of – just one more crowded street at night. Something seething and enclosed about it, centuries of vice and money coagulated between the rather beautiful tall houses.

Our leaders stopped at a certain doorway on the left. We went up a steep, circular, rather dark stone staircase that twisted round to the front of the house, and went into a small bare room. We six and the cinema manager (his bodyguard stayed below) sat on cushions at the end facing the window. There wouldn't have been room for more people. Two male musicians sat on the floor just inside the window, one with a small drum, the other a flute. A girl sat on the ledge of the open window, her back to the street below. The remaining central area – not much – was the stage for the dancer. Her trousers and tunic were not spectacular, she was not beautiful. The cinema manager handed round wadges of small notes, and we were shown how to tuck them into different parts of our own and each other's clothing – collar, pockets, hair, clothing, shoes, belt – this game can be developed indefinitely.

Then the musicians started to play, and the dancer put anklets with bells on her feet. Suddenly she began to dance. It was as if a steel spring had been loosed, fantastic muscular energy exploding into life. But it was much more; irresistible grace, a more than human fluidity; water would dance like that. Her whole body moved, she used what floor space there was, often very swiftly, but she didn't seem to need more. Though the dance was consistent, it had great variety. Her arms moved all the time, but as a part of the whole body. Every now and then she made a quick pounce on one of the little tufts of money placed for her in someone's clothing, snatched it and tucked it into her own clothing, and tweaked an ear, a nose, hair. Her approaches were almost frightening with the sense of latent strength; in fact, there was something dangerous in her whole personality and dance; when she was dancing, she was absolutely dominant. Her dancing was mesmeric; flowing yet startling with changes of pace.

At last we went down the dark steep stairs out to the street again. Further along we turned into another door, up another steep staircase and sat in another small room to watch the second dancer. Basically similar but interpreted by a different personality as well as a different body. Again one was loth for it ever to stop, but we thought the first more powerful, more vivid. These are professional dancers, not prostitutes, though living in that street. They can and do command extremely large sums to dance at private parties. If they were ever persuaded to dance in Western cities, they would triumph.

The street was quieter when we came out, and darker, as more shutters were closed, and fewer lit windows still framed the painted dollies. A *tonga* drawn by a light grey pony was waiting for its fare to return. A white cow had settled for the night against the house where the tonga waited. She lifted her head, and the pony slowly dropped his, until their noses all but touched. The two pale animals held their conversation, a moment of gentleness in that harsh place.

When we got back to the square outside the cinema, one of our cars had a flat tyre, and the two bodyguards changed it with lightning speed – what a useful get-away team they would make! Inside the cinema the same film was still unfolding.

Again the little PIA linked the country. We flew into

Peshawar at dusk. A tapestry of history and fiction hung in the back of one's mind behind this legendary North West Frontier, Ghengis Khan and Tamburlaine and Alexander, the Moguls, the Hindus, the British. I had read in my *Pakistan Times* that day that already there was a refugee problem from Afghan tribesmen beginning to move through the Khyber for fear of the growing Russian presence in their country (the actual invasion was some months ahead). We had booked rooms at Deans, a famous old hotel, but it proved too much even for us; a chain of bare rooms – sitting-room, bedroom, dressing-room, bathroom (more than usually flooded): a shaking battle to open or close any drawer in the gimcrack furniture. But what really overwhelmed one with depression was the position of the tiny windows, high up against the ceiling, so that you felt in prison.

We moved to the Intercontinental, to a charmingly appointed bedroom with a wide view over their garden. Unfortunately, a smell of drains became apparent the second day, at first faint, but growing steadily. Not from the bathroom, the one place it didn't penetrate. We decided it came through the air-conditioning vent. As I kept waiting for it to disappear, and as we were out all the time, I didn't mention it to the pleasant and efficient young manager. The day we left it had spread to the whole corridor. I thought the manager had enough on his hands. If we wanted a light lunch in the attractive dining-room, we could not order from the menu because 'the kitchen staff are at Prayers'. It seemed an unfortunate time for an hotel. True, there was a line of dishes laid out to choose from, but they were all the dishes of clarified fat and little peppers we were surfeited with, and would be eating in the evening anyhow. (No wonder every man over middle age seemed to have had open-heart surgery. No wonder yoghourt was considered a necessity on every table.)

We hired a car, with a very pleasant Pathan driver called Abdullah, and the three of us were a happy party of explorers for quite a long time. First, of course, to the Khyber, through the suburbs of Peshawar, through the flat green tilled country, until the road began to wind up into the tribal lands. No one, no race in history, has ever ruled these tribesmen. *Yaghistan*, meaning 'land of the unruled', the early Moslem conquerors called them. The present arrangement is that the law of the Pakistan government prevails on the road; murder or robbery (the traditional way of life), if committed on the road, can in theory be punished. But one step off the road and you are in the tribal lands and there is no law but theirs. This is worth bearing in mind should you be ill-informed enough to try and photograph (or even look at) a woman. Every man and boy carries a gun. 'A boy would rather starve than not have a gun. To show that you can protect yourself is more important than food.' These are proud races of great antiquity – the Afridis, the Orksa, the Khattah, the Maksud. Sometimes one of them will leave the tribal lands and enter the general life of Pakistan. I had sat next to such a one at a luncheon party Begum Noon had given in Rawalpindi, and he had outlined for me the areas of the different groups, and their relationships with each other. But it was from a Pathan in Peshawar I learned that these great sealed mud-brick buildings – houses, castles, villages – with heavy metalled doors and crenellated walls, which we drove past for miles on either side of the road, were furnished inside with sophisticated treasures like a rich house in Peshawar; curtains, carpets, pictures, furniture, glass. It is in this area that the refugees from Afghanistan were already beginning to pitch their tents.

We had been told that we should go up to the Khyber on the train. *The* train. The famous train which runs every Friday, whose line, a breathtaking piece of engineering, had been built by the British in 1925. I'm glad to say wiser counsel prevailed – you saw the train much better if you went up by car and waited for it to appear at strategic points. Also its time of departure was uncertain (though other people said this was a calumny and you could tell the time by it!) but it was undoubtedly slow, sooty, and crowded.

So where the road was a serpent coiling through grey rocks and shale, the bare craggy land tumbling in stones endlessly on either side, and dotted with little stone-built *piquets*, we waited.

These *piquets* – four walls with embrasures – were still in excellent condition and I sat in the shade of one, on the steep hillside. We waited an hour for the train to complete a course which would bring it only three miles higher. A distant puff of smoke announced its presence emerging from a tunnel, then its disappearing into the next long tunnel. Then we could hear the pistons pounding, desperate with effort, the black clouds of smoke marking the course as the train looped and looped. Then a shrill triumphant whistle, and smoke nearer on the tortuous but implacable climb upwards. And at last she came, emerging miraculously from the rocks like an animal coming out of its hole. She had an air of proud achievement; she had done it again! She was like Queen Victoria, stout, a bit breathless, very sure of herself; dignified, unstoppable.

The train was so full that every coach overflowed with tribesmen, all, it seemed, waving guns – there was no room for them except by holding them out of the windows or over the top of the open trucks.

The rear engine took the load as the train switched direction and chugged on; we lost it round a bend, but could follow its course by emerging puffs of smoke, and later we met it again.

We went first to the Khyber accompanied by a young man working for Begum Noon's newly-born tourist organisation, and appreciated all he told us of the history-soaked frontier. But we went again with just Abdullah, so we could look, and think, and remember.

First stop is Jamrud, for the Guard Post; we wait in the car while Abdullah goes in to show the car's papers and pay toll (the inevitable slight nervousness, will anything be wrong?). Two guards come out and peer at us, and at the inside of the car, but finally wave us on. The village street is wide and alive and moving, brilliantly massed painted buses, booths selling food, plastic goods, spare parts; a few dogs, goats everywhere, chickens. Everyone wears rifles as part of their clothing.

The village ends with a great modern stone arch across the road; the beginning of the Khyber. On the left, just through the arch, a line of marble tablets each outlining one of the invasions which have passed this way. The Persians, the Greeks, the Parthians, the Moguls, the Sikhs, the British. On to Shagrai Fort, piled up solid and red on the left (still a manned military post). Then, further on, the strange little British Cemetery, strange because so small and unfinished, terraced above the road. Only about twelve graves, most had died of cholera in 1919, one in action, one *drowned*. Where were all the others?

Then the Pass narrows to a deadly bottleneck, and where it opens out there is the triangular plain on which every invading force – Moguls, Sikhs, British – camping for the night in the first open space, had been slaughtered by the Afridis.

Over the stony plain to Landi Kotal, with bazaars steep on the hillside. Landi Kotal, bustling and booming, the tall buildings on either side of the narrow sharply-sloping streets closely barred. For the industry here is smuggling. An industry of £100 million a year. By an agreement with Afghanistan, goods coming into Karachi by sea can be taken in bond to Torkhan, the border post between Pakistan and Afghanistan. From there they are smuggled over the Khyber to Bara for distribution, not only throughout Pakistan, but to India as well. Ah, but you need a pass to enter Bara, with its great walled supermarket enclaves. What do you want? St Michael clothes? Refrigerators, electric cookers, glass, china, new tyres? This is a very sharply run business, the Torkhan to Bara smuggling route. You see mounds of goods moving slowly along mountain tracks and realise that under each load there is a mule. But motor transport is necessary too, there are some things even an Afridi smuggler cannot put on a mule, and here the risk is greater, though incredible journeys are made to by-pass the road. 'We catch about fifty per cent,' a police chief told us. 'But even so, the profits are so tempting it's worth it for the other fifty per cent.'

Torkhan is a triangle of bright emerald green, visible from afar, the other end of the Khyber, and beyond lies the dazzling white crown of the Hindu Kush. Just a pole across the road, a Pakistan border guard on one side, an Afghan guard on the other. We watched the Afghans streaming across in little groups, going home laden. Sacks of corn, bundles, a lot of machinery, black goats. They are animated, powerful, wiry dark men, always talking, exuding enormous energy. How far will they walk? One feels that for ever would not be too far. One man is leading a black nanny-goat on a string, he carries one very small kid, and the next in size keeps close beside the mother, but two bigger ones keep straying from side to side of the road and are always being shooed back.

'They show no papers,' Ralph said. 'They just chat with the guards.'

'Yes!' Abdullah told us. 'That is the check! The guards know their accent. Anyone who spoke differently would be stopped.'

The Russians had built a two-mile tunnel through the Hindu Kush – of doubtful military value as a well-placed bomb could block it, but a marvellous way to infiltrate people.

Every evening in Peshawar, I went out on to our balcony when I had dressed for the evening's diversions, and looked at the vast Mogul fort humped solid and secret against the sunset, and remembered it had been the headquarters from which our friend Rahim, as a young Brigadier, had commanded the whole Iran, Afghanistan, China, Russia border. The only period when the whole frontier had been under one command. Our gentle-speaking, smiling, very lively-minded host, who had fetched me from the hairdresser in Karachi! – I was very honoured. His comment on the brooding Russian presence then looking towards the Khyber, was that if the tribesmen were equipped with telescopic rifles, they might form a very persistent obstacle. This was something they had never had. Their guns now as always were manufactured in Darra, a demonically busy village where gun-making is the cottage industry; men and boys sit in the road, in barns, in their own houses, all, every one, working at the making of every kind of gun (down to ball-pen pistols). They use any metal they can get. Their guns had at certain moments of history been in advance of ours, and never far behind. But they had never had telescopic lenses. With them, in their own protective rocks, with the agility, eyesight, and the marksmanship bred in them and practised ever since they could walk, they could, on the David and Goliath principle, still be formidable.

Indeed, a little later, after the Russian invasion of Afghanistan, I read Afghan guerrillas had seriously harassed the Soviet armour, though the Afghans have neither the territory, the tradition nor the guns of the tribesmen of the Khyber Pass.

Of course we walked again and again in the bazaars of Peshawar, perhaps a wilder labyrinth than the bazaars of Lahore, Pindi, or Karachi. I think they are more spectacular, the high white houses with elaborate balconies are exquisite if you can safely stop for a moment to look up from the maelstrom of the shouting streets. The smell of the food cooking over braziers in shallow steaming pans is delicious. The piled fruit and vegetables blaze with colour, the sweet shops look so enticing one must go in and buy some of this, some of that – and some of those little green ones – and what are those pink squares? Sampling our little bags, out in the street again, was disappointing, as they all taste the same and have little flavour, just sweet. The shops of nuts and kernels I could never pass. The colour of the crowds is negative, the clothes neutral fawns and greys, pale, dust-coloured. Only the faces flash and sparkle and laugh and shout. The movement of people and bicycles and ponies and donkeys and occasional cars make walking in the bazaars exhausting. One finds a quiet side-alley and draws

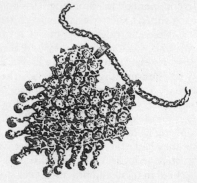

breath as behind a breakwater, then plunges back into the rough sea. In the larger towns the butchers' shops are together in one street, so fortunately avoidable, as they all hang up large sheets of white membrane criss-crossed with blood, which are particularly nauseating.

The gold and silver bazaars of Peshawar are famous – and very expensive. (Those in Pindi are too extensive to examine.) We wanted a few little presents, and walked the length of this street several times. A steep step runs along each side, and on top of it the shop-owners sit at little tables, their small crowded shops behind them, massed with silver, and occasionally gold, jewellery. The most superior shops have their best things in glass cases, and do not tout for custom, but eye one speculatively. The slightly less selective shops accost violently. 'What you want? What you look for? Very rare, very old.' There are indeed fascinating things, at a price, but they need searching out of the masses of filigree, the piles of chains. We marked down two pendants and some old silver anklets. A cripple squirmed after us seated on the ground, propelling himself along by his arms, singing and begging. His faint and plaintive song pursued us as we moved up and down the street. Whenever we paused, there he was. Stopping to examine one of the pendants I saw a lump

of feathers tucked beside the feet of the shop-owner. Climbing up the steep step to pass him and look inside the shop, I realised it was a chicken, alive, its feet tied together, lying on its side waiting till the end of the day when, swung by the string round its feet, it would be carried home and at last killed. I would never have imagined it possible that the eye of a chicken could express such infinite endurance. On the far side of the step, between the street and the shop, ran an open sewer.

If a man shopper returns later without a woman, he may get a little off the price, but bargaining is not a normally accepted custom here, the asking price really does relate to what they expect to get. If you don't buy it someone else will, another day. There is no hurry, they are very rich – the smallest booth will change hands for not less than the equivalent of £2500. Incidentally, I never saw another white face in the bazaars of any city.

When we were in Karachi, two months before, a lifetime ago! worlds away, we had been invited to a wedding if we could be in Peshawar at this time – a three-day Muslim wedding. We had dined at the house a few days before, the home of the bride-groom's parents, a large white house standing back in its garden of trees. A lusciously lovely hostess who was of Sind in this country of Pathans! Her husband, tall and ramrod straight, an ex-general, was quiet, while she more than held her own in political argument across the dinner table – if 'political' covers a whole way of life and customs. Her pretty daughter had just come back from America, where she had been a student. 'What a different world!' I said to her mother, chatting one morning over fruit salad with pepper. 'Yes,' my hostess said, 'I went to the States to visit her. She kept all those attractive young men at arm's length. Really, if I'd been her age I don't think I'd have been so strong-minded! I asked her – why don't you go out with these nice boys? and she said, "Oh, mother, what's the point? There could never be anything in it. I could never marry anyone here. Not till I come home."'

'Is this being Muslim?' I asked.

'No, I don't think it's that so much as the family. It's very strong with us. The sense of being a part of the family, of belonging.'

I had been invited that morning to see the bride's jewels and saris, a woman's function. I was shamefully late, because we had been again to the Khyber, but she said, 'Never mind. The ladies have all seen them and are having coffee, but I will show you the jewels.' We went to her bedroom, and sitting on the side of her bed she opened all the boxes. Each contained a full set – in rubies, in emeralds – consisting of necklace, ear-rings, bracelets, rings, sometimes hair ornaments. I remembered my mother telling me, when I was a small child, that at the Durbar the Indian princes were dripping with fabulous jewels, but uncut, so that to Western eyes they lacked brilliance. Now these, still, were uncut, so the ones I thought most beautiful were the turquoise set, enormous turquoises of superb colour; and one set all in gold, exquisitely worked. When she had put the boxes in a cabinet and locked it, she led me to another room to see the saris, each laid out on its own chair. Gold, the colour of weddings, predominated, each sari embroidered with a different colour. Then one entirely in gold, which was the wedding sari.

The evening of the wedding Ralph and I were separated, I was fetched in the largest and best appointed car I have ever seen – a Mercedes – you could have lived in it, like a house, and driven by the largest chauffeur (large in height and muscle, not fat); chauffeur, bodyguard? Ralph would be fetched later to the bridegroom's house for a stag party. We were supposed to be leaving Peshawar in the morning, but didn't quite know when we should meet again, as the beginning of events was clear but the end seemed indefinite.

As we turned in at the gate, I saw the whole lawn in front of the house was covered by a huge marquee – not white, but in soft colours that blended with the garden. We stopped in the drive, which was full of people splendidly dressed, all moving about, there was a great sense of bustle and excitement.

A nephew of the family was waiting for me, I had met him at previous parties. 'I am deputed to welcome you, which is a great pleasure.' The daughter of the house whom I knew best was beside me. 'This is my sister, this is my aunt, you remember her? and another aunt, and this is my half-sister. This is my grandmother, and this is my half-sister's aunt ...' I realised the relationships were more important than the names (and even harder to remember). 'Now we wait for the presents – the bridegroom's presents to his bride, they must go in first.'

We all waited at the side of the drive. Coloured lights flickered over the women's faces, all crowded together, so many of them beautiful, all animated and vivid, flashing eyes and a miasma of jewels and a haze of golden clothes against the dark green hedge, and flowers on which the lights blazed then vanished to blackness as someone moved in front of the light. The drive was wet, there had been heavy rain, and people's sandals slipped in the gravel. The lights, always coming and going as people moved across them, turned the jewel-decked heads into a kaleidoscope. I thought, 'This indeed is the fabulous East! The glamorous Orient, the legend come to life. I have never seen anything like this, never imagined anything like this. And it is quite real.'

Then a bustle and a stir and all heads turned to the gate. The bridegroom and a few other men – relatives – came up the drive almost at a run, carrying covered baskets. 'His gifts to his bride. They are mostly fruit and cakes,' someone whispered to me. 'They are symbolic, everything is very symbolic.' The little procession turned into the garden, into the great tent, and we all followed. I found my friend, the daughter of the house, beside me. 'I will take you to my mother, she is asking for you.' How they managed to find me, let alone remember my existence, in such a crowd, I shall never know, and look after me so exquisitely.

This indeed was the family. There were three hundred at a rough estimate, I was told, mostly women, the men were at the bridegroom's house. 'But there *are* a few men?' I said. 'Yes, the bridegroom has a few relations and special friends to support him.' I was conscious of a maze of rich blurred colours under the coloured lights. 'We are not supposed to decorate like this under the new austerity laws,' my hostess said. 'But ...'

146

Several rows of chairs ran the length of the wedding tent, as in a theatre, facing a little fire on the ground, and the gifts had been placed round it. Several servants were lying on the floor tending the fire, but gossamer saris kept floating past it, which seemed terrifyingly dangerous. I sat beside my hostess – though everyone kept moving about, to talk to as many people as possible. She was always lovely, but in her wedding gold she was breathtaking. You must wear gold at a wedding, even if it means buying yards of gold ribbon and sewing it on to existing clothes. Here the room swirled with every shade from pale wheat to dark copper, sometimes based on a colour, green or crimson or apricot. Chains of jewels were festooned up from ear-rings into black hair. Three or four necklaces, gold chains with jewels, a load of bracelets, rings on every finger. Worn by different women, in a different setting, it would have been too much, and spoiled the effect. But on these sinuous dark women, who seem to be in a state of continuous movement like butterflies – wrapped in their silks and gauzes – they shimmer and glow in the memory.

A few women wore a hand-ornament consisting of fine chains running from a bracelet to a ring on every finger, almost a dainty hand-armour. 'Yes, they are very rare,' someone told me. 'She must have inherited it, she is very lucky.'

An older lady, one of the grandmothers, came and talked to me. She wore black, being in mourning, but it was threaded with gold. 'I have come from . . .' and she mentioned somewhere far away. 'I have a virus. I am so full of antibiotics I am barely conscious.' I said it was good of her to come, and she said – not censoriously, but as if explaining a happy thing, 'Oh, no! I had to come. Of course. I would have come if I was dying. The whole family is here. We are gathered for the wedding of one of us, it is a great event. We are all one, you see, that is what this ceremony means. We are each a part of the whole. That is our strength. It is a wonderful thing, a wonderful feeling. You are never alone, you are not just one. You are a part of the family.'

Then the bridegroom and a little procession of his friends danced round the fire. Then they disappeared. The throng behind the fire grew dense. 'The bride will come through that door on the left. He will be waiting for her, and the ceremony will take place. Look, that is the bride's mother, sitting there, do you see?'

I wondered how well, if at all, the bride and groom knew each other, but answers were vague and contradictory. 'Oh, yes. He is a friend of her brothers' so she would have seen him when he came to their house to see her brothers.' Someone told me it was not considered a particularly good match, but 'They kept offering him girls, and this was the only one he would look at, so . . .'

I tried very hard to find out what was happening, but everyone who began to explain was distracted by some long-unseen relative. I glued my eyes to the throng behind the fire. Some professional dancers came and danced round the fire, among the baskets of gifts, the flowers and the fruit. ('Ah, but you should see the dancers of Lahore!' I heard someone say.)

'When will the ceremony happen?' I asked.

'Oh, it is over. Did you not see? It is too crowded, she has gone now, the bride.'

There had been no moment when the movement and talk had been less, and the tight-packed crowd of close relations had hidden everything. Is it possible that the getting-together of the family, everyone greeting as many others as possible – this expression of solidarity – was what they had come for, more than to watch the actual ceremony?

Everyone began to get up and move into another tent for dinner. This too was softly lit by coloured lights, and the enormous carpeted floor was dotted with metal tripods holding shallow trays of glowing coals, and over the heat were the dishes in metal bowls – all the spicy mixtures of meat and vegetables in different sauces. The lovely ladies were good trenchermen and ate vigorously, standing in little groups round the braziers.

Then we moved on to a covered verandah for tea and cakes. This seemed to me a transition to another world. I heard one woman say to another, 'Are you cold? I'm freezing.' I wondered if the new 'austerity laws' had affected this part of the evening. The other new, or re-emphasised, laws did not seem to bother people unduly. ('All those lashes for adultery? ... 'Yes, but there must be five witnesses. It is not usual to commit adultery before five people.')

Going home in the great Mercedes I thought of this strange, strong network of the family, stronger than religion or politics. We had talked at several parties to the nephew of one of our hosts – a soldier, ex-Sandhurst, also a politician. He and Vicki Noon were the only two people we met whom I felt really believed in and were working for the future of their country. Most seemed to be waiting to see what happened, hoping to survive and preserve their way of life. He had spent fourteen months in the condemned cell of one of Bhutto's prisons (next-door to the execution cell, and hearing what happened). He had fought an election from there – and won! – because they had underestimated his following, so didn't print enough votes against him. So, he was sent out in a van with two guards, at night, into open country, then told to get out. He walked away, his back prickling. After a long conversation between his two guards, they told him to come back and get in the van again. They explained that their orders had been to shoot him 'trying to escape'. But they had just heard Bhutto had fallen, so weren't sure if the order still held, and decided to play it safe. He was released the next day. But his uncle, in whose house we were talking, had, over the same period, been one of Bhutto's ambassadors, recalled when he fell.

'But surely – being on opposite sides – must have divided families?' I asked.

'Yes, it did,' he answered.

'Yet here we are in your uncle's house?'

'Life must go on.'

'And what next, for you?'

'The next thing for me, I think, is that I must fight another election. Not from prison this time, I hope!'

From what I read in the papers, he has not yet had the opportunity.

We longed to see at least the foothills of the Himalayas, but the snow had come lower, and lain longer that year than anyone could remember. Swat and Gilgit had been cut off until nearly the time of our departure. The manager of the airline, knowing it was our last chance, kindly gave us his personal tickets on the second plane to Gilgit after the flight became possible.

I am glad to have flown over even the fringe of that awful roof of the world. The Himalayas were the last of the world's great mountain ranges which I had not seen. For the first time I really understood Malory's words explaining why he had to climb Everest 'because it is there'. Anyone feeling challenged by that personality would indeed be under a spell. All mountains have their own character – the human-haunted Atlas, the empty Rockies, the clean glistening mountains of Norway, the Alps, the Andes. But the Himalayas seem terrible beyond comprehension; they do not relate to people or to life at all – yet they themselves are alive in a way other mountains are not, and hostile. And I have only seen the tiny edge of that implacable white other-world.

We had only a few hours in Gilgit, the little aircraft was under pressure, people who lived there had been cut off for so long. It was early spring up here, the almond and apricot blossom was just beginning, and the first green. From here you could see Rakaposhi, one of the greatest peaks. We passed the original

polo ground, where a very embattled form of the game is still played. We were driven through the town to a new motel, a row of pleasantly appointed bungalows now empty, just completed, hoping to start a summer season. We sat under a flowering tree in the garden and the manager gave us coffee. He showed us some big publicity photographs they had taken. 'We have rare and interesting fauna up here, you know!' First a bird. Then a magnificent picture of a snow leopard. 'We have snow leopards in our mountains! They have become very rare now. We had a cub here recently. We sent it to the Lahore Zoo!'

So...This is where he had come from. This is where he should be, growing up in those wild mountains where the spring was beginning, with one of his own kind, leaping among the sharp rocks in the snow and the blossom and the sun. Instead, he would spend all his life alone in that concrete cage – 'air-conditioned'.

At the airstrip there was a slight hold-up. Throughout Pakistan at this time passengers and their luggage were searched before every internal flight. I always found the women who searched the women to be quick, thorough and courteous. But! Here there was no woman. In vain I pointed out that I had no luggage, only my handbag which anyone could look at, and they could see what I was wearing. It would not do. Regulations must be observed. The manager of the airport rushed off, the plane waited. He came back with a startled lady hastily adjusting her black *burka* over her face, and she and I withdrew to a little booth where she opened my handbag and ran the X-ray over me. I ran to the aircraft and we took off.

Our last journey with Abdullah and his car was up to Swat, hoping to penetrate from there further into the mountains. We drove through fields of opium poppies and apricot blossom, stopping to climb up to a spreading fortification of Buddhist ruins at Takht-i-Bhai. Above and just beyond the town of Swat stands a hotel, once a British hill station. Banks of violets in the garden, and the first roses. A long walk along shining ivory-coloured soap-stone verandahs; one could imagine the rows of heavy old wooden deck-chairs with long footstools that once stood here. Our bedroom and sitting-room had not, I think, been altered since those days, certainly the bathroom hadn't. I suppose this plumbing – even a shower! – had once been the height of modern luxury. Two small chamber-pots with lids stood behind the lavatory. They were the colour of verdigrised copper, but I did not investigate closely. The lights in the sitting-room were so weak and high it was impossible to read. The hotel was almost empty, the food in the dining room uneatable. The flat roof of this extraordinary building was also of shining soap-stone, and big enough to parade half a Division. We waited there one night to see the moon rise over the mountains. It came up blurred, through cloud. One thought of the people of one's race who had filled this place, this remote place so far from home; in this deeply loved country, but still so far from home. The only link, in those days before aeroplanes and radio, the great ships which plied to and fro. The voyage which could not be shortened no matter what urgency of illness or death drove one. No wonder those ships became such known personalities, with character and a mystique of their own.

Abdullah drove us along a ravine into the mountains, with rocks rising steeply on the left and a river course on the right, many glaciers pouring down to it from the mountains above, the discoloured ice cut off like an untidy cake above the river. We wanted to reach Chitral Province, which occupies the extreme north-west corner of Pakistan, dominated by the Hindu Kush. We were only a few miles away, when we came upon stopped trucks, and looking past them, saw that an avalanche had come down across the road. It stretched for a long way. Already a lot of men were working to clear it; a line of black midgets bowing before the enormous snow. They certainly wouldn't be through today.

We and the trucks backed till it was possible to turn, then started back to Swat, meeting others who turned back too, so that when we reached the narrow Malakand Pass (scene of a famous battle) we were in quite a congestion of traffic, and I realised I was smitten with both sickness and diarrhoea. I so seldom have anything the matter with me – why, when I do, is it always in the most public and melodramatic circumstances? Abdullah, with instant tact and skill, manoeuvred his car to the side of the road away from the precipice on to the stony slope, so I could get out and stumble up the hill to a little shelter of rocks.

It was a grim ending. The unforgiving mountains standing behind the teeming confused country. Never in its history, under any name, any rule, has it had a long enough period of peace to plan, only to survive. More than once we had heard the phrase, said smilingly, 'Ah, the golden days of our slavery!' (under the British). Abdullah said to us, 'My father tells me the British treated all men equally. It is not so now.' He had seven children and hoped for more. Pakistan has the biggest population increase in the world, and seeing what happened to Indira Ghandi and her son when they tried to limit their population, no politician dares touch the subject. Yet the vitality of the people explodes from every bazaar. Will things ever be different here? It has been said, 'Pakistan is not a poor country, it is just a country in which many people are poor.' The Indus plain is the most fertile land in the world. In Islamabad we met two young men who had started a Museum of handcrafts and regional embroideries. They had travelled the country very cheaply, camping, and buying when and where they found treasures. Their collection was a glorious demonstration of skill, beauty and variety – recent, before you start on the infinite store of antiquity! At the moment their collection is housed in two bare rooms, but they hope soon to move into fine permanent premises. Hope! Hope! One of these young men said, 'Bhutto promised us three things. Food, houses and education. He was tackling the first two, he was not given time for the third.' But other people said, 'Those houses were never built. Only promised.' Who had said to us, 'In our country the buck never stops passing.'

Our last night, the last dinner party, we met another High Court Judge, also an impressive personality, and easy to talk to. I asked him why, after quite a long time in the country, listening to so many people talk – not just to us but among themselves – I heard so much about the present and the past, hardly anything about the future?

He answered with a question, 'Are you a student of Chekhov?'

I was taken aback for a moment. 'Yes, yes – I think so. Oh, I see what you mean.'

His aquiline face softened into a smile. 'We talk, talk! We don't *do*.'

Part IV

WALES

The Story of Gilfachwen

'GILFACHWEN MEANS long, white and narrow', they told us. No trace of whitewash remained, but the little ruined hill farm was certainly long and narrow.

Some time later another friend, and one more closely connected with the house said, 'No, no! White is correct, but "Gilfach" means a valley, a cleft, a narrow place, it couldn't possibly refer to the house, it must refer to the place it's built in, the country round it.'* This was difficult to apply, as the house is backed by a line of hills, and looks over rolling country to distant ranges. Perhaps it is useless to try and pin down ancient

---

* Later, we were there when Wales had the worst floods in twenty years, and the stream that flows down the hill beyond the house became much too big for its culvert, and flowed down our road, making Gilfachwen a moated house for two days. The gush of water, a high wave, was long, white and narrow. This could be visible for miles, and in the past, before there were culverts, would have happened far more frequently. Could this – a landmark and sign in time of floods – by any chance be the origin of the name?

names in countries with a different language – better just to wait for understanding to emerge.

The land in which Gilfachwen stands had been bought for us in a snowstorm while we were in Australia. We had owned forestry in this part of Wales for twenty years, and come to love the country. This high saucer in the hills (its name, Panteg, means Lovely Valley) was particularly wild and beautiful. It joined one of our original plantations, Ralph had left instructions that if it ever came on the market, he would like to bid for it.

The deeds told us our new property contained three small farms and a line of hill fields behind. As we never afforest agricultural land, we planned to sell these. Eight months passed before we could come and look at them, and – mercifully! they hadn't been sold. This was perhaps not surprising as one of them had fallen down, one was described as being in 'very poor condition', only one was immediately saleable, and as well as being remote and lonely even for that country, the private road, our road leading to them, was pretty rough in places.

I can't remember what time of year we first saw it, as it is now so saturated with all seasons, but I think it was a quiet green day of full summer that we headed the car up to that distant stronghold of mountains and finally, at a thousand feet, turned off the public road between two hillocks that seem to guard the entrance, opened a bent metal gate, looped on to the gate-post with the coarse fraying pink string which ties every gate in rural Wales, and dipped down into the 'lovely valley'. I know we left the car and went on foot the first time, not sure what we should find. Ground rising on the right, falling away on the left, sheep grazing, flickers of gorse still, stone walls upholstered with moss and heather and bilberry, ferns and harebells and foxgloves, topped with rowan and beech and ash and laburnum.

The first farmhouse, standing above the road on the right, was in good condition, except that vandals had thrown out the cooker and smashed the light above the porch, as well as breaking windows; why come so far, along a track that led nowhere, and then savage the place? Electricity had been

brought as far as this house, we noted, the transformer stood in a field just below the road. A few fields further on – the track bending, so each was hidden from the other – we came upon the second farmhouse. This was just broken walls of superb stones, quite big it must have been, collapsed into grass and nettles and old fruit bushes, set in some magnificent trees.

Still the road continued – quite a good road in the main, only one or two soft spots. Then a dog-leg bend up to the right, a widening, with one tall monolith of a stone gate-post, the other lost, and then the road ran straight up to the third house, Gil-fachwen. This was the end of the road, beyond this our forestry. The house looked very long and low, buried in undergrowth, two grand and enormous beech trees beside it, completely dominating it. An ivy tree smothered the southern end, climbing and flowering right over the chimney, and a colony of rooks inhabited this, rising and swirling and cawing as we drew up.

Why, then, did it have this air of welcome, of tranquility, of pleasure, an air of occasion, as though one had indeed arrived somewhere? It seemed to be waiting for people, expecting someone to come. If a house could be said to smile, it smiled.

Picking your way through grass and nettles and stones over the mound on which it stood, you could peer in through each of the deep-set square windows at the dim interior. The partition between the two rooms was broken, the floor deep in rubble and plaster and sheep's wool; an old bucket, one boot, bits of an iron bedstead, a frying pan by the fireplace; the usual debris of an abandoned cottage.

These objects became very familiar, as each time we went to Wales we visited the house and looked in. At last I lifted the bent nail that served for a latch, moved the stone and eased the door open wide enough to go inside. I went in alone. Ralph was walking a further plantation to inspect the growth-rate of trees, any necessary drainage, the state of the fences. I wanted to see how the house felt. It felt like a lived-in cottage, not lonely at all. The little curving staircase was crumbling, but just possible to climb. The windows, square and deep like those downstairs, came at waist-height. The floor was sagging and broken, you could see through to the downstairs. The chimney-stack running up through the centre of the house had holes in it.

Two rooms up, two down and a cow byre, that was the house. But four walls of pearly-grey flat stones two-and-a-half feet thick stood strongly, only cracking where the ivy tree had penetrated. And the personality of the house was intact. Arriving there one had an extraordinary feeling of peace and happiness, a lifting of the spirit. At the back there was the little horseshoe-shaped garden usual in this area, circled with a stone wall and a ring of trees – cherry, apple, laburnum, ash, a huge patch of snowdrops and, later, daffodils of a variety I had never seen before. Someone had loved this house. Someone should live here again.

We'd always dreamed of making a pied-à-terre in one of our Welsh woods, instead of staying at a pub when it was necessary to visit them. For many years now the Dolaucothi at Pumpsaint had become very homelike to us, and the people who ran it, Glyn and Diana Cooley, had become friends. But the idea of a forestry house persisted, and we had left an acre unplanted at the entrance to one plantation in case we ever wanted to build there, and had regretted it when vandals wrecked an old RAF watchtower and hut in another. In either of these places we should have had nothing at all to start from. Whereas here, we had to upgrade the road for purposes of forestry work and extraction, which brought Gilfachwen into the realm of practical possibility. 'It would be fun to make this over,' I said to Ralph.

As I'd said this about countless ruins all over Europe from Corsica to Greece, he didn't take much notice. But our forestry manager who was with us on one occasion – I said it every time we went there – remarked; 'If you should ever want an architect, there's a very good one in Carmarthen,' and a young forester who was also with us said, 'They knew where to build, the old people! On rising ground, sheltered from the north and east, facing to the south and west . . .' He stepped back to glance up the hill for the course of the stream that flowed past the far side of the house, 'You'd have no problem about water. And you've got the electricity as far as your other farm.'

Two or three hundred years old, they thought.

When we first planted in Wales, we'd heard there was hostility to English people owning forestry. I think this was really that anyone – everyone – hates an absentee landlord, strangers invading and using their land. But we were not strangers. From the beginning we had enjoyed getting to know the hill farmers whose land marched with ours. They'd got used to us over the years, Ralph driving his exotic cars, me in a headscarf beside him and a black Alsatian in the back, nosing round the narrow winding roads where everyone is known and noticed. We liked chatting, leaning over a gate discussing the season, the sheep, the dogs. 'Best sheepdog I ever had was half Alsatian. This one with me now is her son, that's quarter Alsatian, he's good too.' We were invited to the annual luncheon of the Brechfa Sheep Dog Trials, and Ralph was asked to make a speech. The ladies wore hats, and I, unprepared, was in my roughest mud-and-rain-clothes. I was ashamed, but they were very kind and understanding.

Anyway, country people are realists. This country had suffered great poverty. Forestry would bring a new industry, developing from the growing of trees to the usage of wood. As a sheep farmer said to us one day, looking at a hill we had ploughed and planted where now the trees were above our heads, 'There's a deal of money now standing on the mountain!'

All this had become a part of our lives. So we *did* go to Carmarthen to see that architect.

Harold Metcalfe was a Yorkshireman who had been practising in London. When he started a family he felt he didn't want to bring them up in a city, and, hearing there was an opening in West Wales for 'an architect who could carry things through', he had moved here. Tall, fair, quite young, with nice offices and considerable panache − all the architects I know are, in different ways, rather colourful and dashing people. I suppose they have to be, to stand up to their clients and protect their designs. So we asked him to come and meet us on the site, and drew him a map of how to find it.

Waiting for him there, I was extremely nervous. He arrived driving a Porsche and dressed in keeping. I was afraid he'd look at our little tumbledown ruin with contempt, and laugh, and say, 'I'll design you a house here with pleasure, but I really think the best thing you can do with this is to pull it down and start again', and I was ready to hackle and snarl in her defence, because already I was becoming involved with her. (The personality of Gilfachwen is feminine; a tough lively Welshwoman of the hills, with that beckoning welcome which had first allured us.)

But he didn't say a word. He sat down on the bank opposite with a light in his eye, got a sketching pad out of his pocket and began to draw.

Much later, Ralph said to him, 'You're obviously doing well, I'm surprised you bother with a little thing like this, and a long journey into the wilds every time you need to see it.' Harold Metcalfe answered, 'This is my fun! Libraries and supermarkets come out of my ears, I can leave them to the office. But this is my fun. This is why I became an architect.'

His plans reached us quite soon. A large book of beautiful drawings, the cover showing a precariously tilted ruin with Ralph and me at each end (both recognisable) trying to prop it up, and a scared Alsatian making off to safety. It was inscribed

'The Gilfachwen Story, or The Innes Folly – A Gripping Story of Intrigue, Treachery and Incompetence Set in the Wild West – by Harold Metcalfe (Dip.)'

The plans were extraordinarily practical and well thought out, and far more ambitious than anything we'd thought of, we studied them with some awe. The drawings were so good they made it all look rather impressive, it was difficult to remember how small it was. But was it? My major contribution had been to say we must take out the remains of the ceiling and not attempt to keep two storeys, as it was impossible to get enough height or light upstairs. Ralph insisted we remove what was left of the wall dividing the downstairs rooms – on either side of the old fireplace – and have just a central fire that you walked all round. This meant almost the whole of the original farmhouse, length, breadth and height, would be one room . . . certainly not small. Metcalfe had clawed light in from every direction; the seven original windows, four down, three up, faced the wide western view. The whole of the short south wall would be one big, tilted window; to the north a door leading to a little paved area had a fanlight as high as itself, to catch light from above the hill. And to the east, three long slashes in the wall faced three long slit windows, almost like big gun embrasures, in the outer wall of the room above. It was very bold, very imaginative. I realised that to flood the place with light from dawn to dusk, in spite of the thickness of its walls and the hill behind it, had been the real challenge to an architect, and what he'd started from, sitting on the bank that first day, sketching. Bulldozing out a margin of the hill at the back and designing the new part was straightforward by comparison.

The skill lay in the smooth welding of old and new. He insisted on a porch ('Why have the rain pouring down your neck when you've lost the key?'). He planned a large storeroom at the back. 'What's that for?' we asked. 'Oh, you'll find plenty.' (We do.) I think they're the only two things he insisted on, and we're very glad he did. Otherwise, he was extraordinarily cooperative to all our ideas, and sparking with ideas of his own. He had designed a staircase to the new upstairs which was like a palisade topped by spears, its flamboyance suited to the proportions of the room. It would be made of wood similar to the wood of the now remote roof.

We had, of course, to get planning permission. Metcalfe's office had, misleadingly, we thought, sent the Council the plans as he had sent them to us, and perhaps the cover-picture set a frivolous aspect on our venture; they turned us down. Ralph and I went to see the planning officer. Unfortunately he was out at a funeral, but we saw his assistant. We explained that we had owned forestry in the area for many years, and kept in regular touch with the work. We had long felt the need of a place of our own, which we could come to at a moment's notice, instead of always having to book ahead into an hotel. Also that we had become very fond of Dyfed; that Ralph was a writer who sometimes needed to get right away to think out some problem in a book.

The whole Council, we heard later, went out to see Gilfachwen, and they decided to give us permission. Indeed, the chairman of the Council kindly wrote and expressed the hope that we would be happy there. The only restriction was that we should not change the appearance and character of the building, and with this we were in strong agreement – looked at across the hills and valleys it would be much the same; you would only see the new part when you walked down the hill behind it.

All this was splendid, but someone had to build it. We needed a builder ... A builder?

Harold Metcalfe tried every builder he'd ever heard of, and then made enquiries far and wide. Nobody was interested. One or two nibbled at the idea, and raised our hopes, but it was too far away. Their men and their transport were more profitably employed nearer home.

Meanwhile, we had put the first house, known as Panteg Farm, to rights and advertised it To Let. We had so many answers, all urgent, some pleading, that I wished we'd had twenty houses to let. We eliminated retired people, weekend people, townspeople who thought they'd like to try a bit of farming, people living alone. We got it down to a short list of three. But one stood out. Short and businesslike, it was signed J. M. Thomas and Ivor Thomas and the address was at Ffarmers. They had been married about nine months, were both working, and at the moment were living in a caravan, 'we haven't had much luck in finding a house.' They would like details as soon as possible. Everything was right. A young couple wanting their first home, belonging not only to the country but to that particular area; they were familiar with its wild high solitude, would have friends and relations in the neighbourhood, so would not be lonely. We went to see Jennifer Thomas: the caravan was on her mother's farm. A notice in the hedge saying 'Milk' and an arrow pointing down a narrow lane. A difficult turning into a farmyard with barns on the right and a house on the left. Her mother was a pretty, animated woman with lovely, pale bracken-coloured hair. Jennifer was taller, bigger built, with black curls and pink cheeks. Half Welsh and half Herefordshire, she looked the traditional Irish Colleen. A firm, composed person, quick and determined. She'd worked in a bookshop and sold Ralph's books, which seemed a good introduction.

Yes, she knew Panteg, she had been brought up in a house only just along the main road from our entrance. After the war Panteg had been farmed briefly by a Pole, then bought from him – for too high a price – by a farmer who worked hard and well to drain, clear and cultivate it. He was spoken of with respect, because he had big ideas and deserved to succeed, but in the end the land defeated him (the hole in an upstairs window was where his wife threw a clock at him 'so they said'). Jennifer's husband, Ivor, was working on the big new dam, and Ralph said he thought it would be nice if we could all meet before anything was decided. So it was arranged they should come down to the Dolaucothi, where we were staying, on a certain evening.

We'd left word they were coming, and thought someone would tell us when they arrived. We finished our dinner – wondering – and went into the bar. It was fairly full, and there, sitting beside the bar, was Jennifer, looking very pretty, with a tall, dark young man who must be Ivor. 'Why didn't you send a message? We didn't know you were waiting – have you been here long?' But they had a glow about them and they were drinking Babycham. We realised they were celebrating their first home. Although Ivor left the talking to Jennifer – he never talks much – there was no doubting he was a positive and likeable personality.

'Who shall I give the key to?' Ralph asked, taking it from his pocket. With great charm she turned to her husband, smiling, and said, 'Oh, to Ivor!' Ralph asked if they'd like to put up a sign saying 'Panteg Farm' where our 'drive', as Jennifer rather grandly called it, left the public road. They looked pleased, and a sign went up very quickly – with a horse's head on it, as Jennifer at that time kept ponies. The dozen or so small steep fields were also let to the Thomases on a separate lease.

We prepared Gilfach' for her future life. Cyrus Williams, our forester, met us there, and we told him exactly which trees we wanted left round the house, beyond it, and approaching it. He marked them so that, when his men were working there on the clearing and drainage necessary before the area opposite could be ploughed and planted, they would know which to leave. Tragically, we had to fell one of the great beech trees beside the house – enormous, hanging right over it, darkening and potentially dangerous. I hoped it would show disease when cut through, thus excusing us, as it was a good age. But the trunk was clean and perfect right through. The stump rises beside the house like a primitive throne, and the enormous trunk, slowly disintegrating, lies below in the field like a fallen gun aimed down the approach road. There were wires from ancient fencing buried deep in the wood, which was why they had not been able to saw it all up. I apologised to that tree before we went away after giving the terrible order, and I apologise still; but what could we do? The second beech, his consort, not quite so huge and a little further away, is now our house tree.

The ivy-tree pulling the corner of the house to pieces was cut and torn off. Ralph had given instructions that a ride, the width of the house, was to be left unplanted through the new forestry sloping away in front of the house, so when the trees grew tall we should not lose the view of the hills. All the new area was now ploughed, drained where necessary and planted.

The whole approach road had to be treated as a main timber extraction road, with the loading-bay just beyond the house (this would give us a nice turn-round for cars outside the garage – if there ever were a garage).

Now when we visited Wales, and came here to see how much of Gilfach' had fallen down, the house above the road, Panteg Farm, had become a home. Ivor was a mechanic – a good one by reputation – and a litter of old cars in various stages of cannibalisation collected round the barn and the cowshed that went with the house. He put in a lot of work to repair the cowshed roof, Jennifer papered the rooms and began a garden. They started a family, a little girl called Gwyneth. They acquired a dog, a cross-bred, half Alsatian, half sheepdog, called Dinah. Her curving run and flattening-to-the-ground approach was sheepdog, but the thick grey coat and shape of the head were Alsatian, though she never quite got her ears up. She was a timid, cringing little thing, Jennifer thought she had not been well-treated – shut up or tied up. She was presumed to be about four.

In the middle of all this Gilfachwen waited, gently disintegrating; waited for a builder. We took down loads of plants and put in. Years passed. The book of plans became one of our souvenirs. Had we been mad enough to think of building a house in the wilds at such a time, with inflation soaring, taxation soaring to lunatic heights; costs soaring? Perhaps it was a merciful release. Gilfach' became a slightly uneasy haunt at the back of our minds.

Whenever we went to Wales to visit our forestry, we always included the Panteg area. Jennifer had flowers in front of her house now, and Gwyneth could wave over the gate. Dinah had gained confidence with good treatment, she no longer cringed. Her Alsatian instinct of protection was developing, and she leapt down from the wall as the car approached. She never became a car-chaser, but no one passed her home unchallenged. As one drove down the deep green lane that widened and opened out in front of the house, that grey shadow would slip into the path and be there waiting. She barked at the car as it passed, then quietly went away. From the first she remembered us, however long between our visits, and greeted us with tremendous friendliness when we were on foot. This did not, of course, affect her self-imposed duty to announce any car, though at either of our voices (if she could hear them above the barking of our own Alsatian, Yiwara, in the back) she generally stopped.

While Ralph and Yiwara went off to walk some area of the woods – to compare the season's growth with our other plantations, check on fencing, see any work that had been done, or needed doing, since our last visit – I would hang about Gilfachwen, slipping in through the gimcrack door, to stand in the rubble and try to relate Metcalfe's drawings to the present reality. I paced out distances, planning the placing of furniture. The cow byre, entered by a big stone doorway (no door) and much frequented by sheep, had some of the finest stonework in the house. It would contain a cloakroom, so we could keep the tiny deepset window, like a porthole, also an entrance lobby and hanging cupboard for rough clothes.

We heard of a builder in Ffarmers, the nearest village. His name was Francis Jones. We examined a line of council houses he was just finishing – very well built. Ralph went to see him. As it was pouring with rain I stayed in the car. 'He's a charming man,' Ralph said when he dripped back. 'I like him – sparkling with intelligence, a good craftsman, I should think. Works with his three sons and one or two others. Talks with real interest about good stonework. I tried him on under-floor central heating and he took it quite calmly – never done it but didn't seem alarmed.'

'But will he do us?'

'He'll think about it. He couldn't take on anything else till the spring.'

Unfortunately, when the spring came he was busy with something else. The autumn was mentioned. Next time we both went to see him. He was certainly a charmer. Vivid dark Welsh face, black hair very slightly grey, warm smile, quick sense of humour. One felt that once he started a difficult job he would see it through. He had lost his wife, and lived with his sons in a nice house he had just built for himself. Almost imperceptibly we realised he had decided to take on the building of Gilfachwen.

By the time he was actually ready to start, we were in Papua New Guinea. This was very fortunate, as it meant Harold Metcalfe fought all the early battles and he and Francis Jones formed a good working relationship. No two men could have been more different – Yorkshireman and Welshman, Saxon and Celt! – but they were both highly intelligent, both took pride and pleasure in their work. Both had their – very different – brands of humour.

Francis Jones had known Gilfach' all his life, but he hadn't seen it for some years, and when he saw its present condition he said, 'Best thing they can do is let me clear all this away and build them a nice modern bungalow!'

Harold Metcalfe agreed it would be a lot easier and cheaper, but it wasn't what we wanted.

When we came back, and in fear and trembling went to see what was happening, we were astounded at the progress. All through a very wet autumn (not, of course, the autumn first thought of) they had toiled to clear it before they could start, load after load of rubble and mess, old rotted partitions, the crumbling staircase, the remains of the two fireplaces. The south end, destroyed by the ivy tree, had been rebuilt to frame the big window. Now we could see the proportions, they were superb. Three tie-beams of very ancient, very simple design, crossed the room at the top of the stone walls. They were called 'crotchers' and were thought to be the oldest form of timber roof support. The men had chopped down one of them before hearing they were meant to be left; so they made an identical replacement, just as their ancestors had made the original ones. The skeleton of the roof was in. Of wood, it would slope right up to the apex.

A ladder made it possible to go upstairs. First the large room into which the staircase would lead, this was the corner of the original house. Then to the right the new part; a landing with a big airing cupboard, bathroom, and our bedroom, to which Ralph had asked for an extra two feet to be added, making it quite a big square room. One saw for the first time how perfect were the views the windows would frame – one on each side. The floors upstairs were wood, downstairs they were red tiles exactly the same as the original ones we'd found under the rubble, and probably made at the same kiln. Below them, the mysterious layer-upon-layer of the heating system.

We came down whenever we could. Now, I stood in the same positions trying to work out how it had been before.

The place seemed alive with men, gradually we got to know them: Francis Jones, of course, with his dark sparkling smile of greeting and general air of everything being under control. There was his very tall son Eirig (or did he only look so tall among the others, short and stocky as Welshmen usually are, mountain people?). He had a shock of black curly hair and a rather enigmatic smile. Then Morgan Lewis and his wheel-barrow, I never saw them apart; he brought the mortar for filling the cracks between the stones, and the plaster for the new part at the back, which was built of breeze blocks. Eirig who put on the mortar and plaster, helped him mix these. Or the barrow would be full of stones, wood, rubble. Morgan seemed per-petually on the move – quite a burly man, he needed to be; dark, of course, not chatty, but liable to surprise you by dropping the odd unexpected crack out of the corner of his mouth.

Denis David was slighter, with a rather puckish face, yet he was the stonemason – a lovely craftsman. I found him inspecting the remaining big stones from the pile beside the house; he looked up and explained, 'I'm looking for a corner-stone. It's very important to have a particularly fine stone for the corner.' Already it was impossible to see where new stoning completed the old, you could only tell by remembering what had been there before.

Francis Jones's other two sons came from time to time, when extra help was needed. A J.C.B. was skilfully driven to bulldoze the extra space at the back, distribute the soil round the house and level where unwanted trees and walls had been. I asked the name of the man who rode so high on this monster, his scarf flying in the wind, who waved so cheerfully when we arrived. 'Ah, that is another Mr Jones!' said Francis.

A magnificent man called Garnet Rees, the blacksmith from Pumpsaint, was making our square central fire basket and the special fittings for the four original square windows downstairs. His smithy was just opposite the Dolaucothi, so we had known him for years.

At first it had startled me when Francis Jones would turn from a discussion with us, and pass on the instructions to his men in Welsh. It was their natural tongue, they always spoke it among themselves, though without thought they spoke in equally perfect English to us – absolutely bilingual. I have never been anywhere else in the world where that could happen (among sophisticates in towns of course, but not among artisans in the mountains). Welsh is spoken all around you in the shops and pubs, except when visitors come in.

Then a second wave of men began to arrive. The plumber; also the electrician, John Edwards, both tunnelling about the house in their mysterious ways. The painter – another Mr Jones – calmly detached from everyone else, made the walls of the new rooms very pale yellow though not as pale as I had wanted, which was a nothing-colour. But it does make the sun always seem to be shining. His painting – not spraying – was perfectionist-smooth.

Francis Jones had made the staircase himself, a superb piece of carpentry, and the design which had seemed so startling in the drawings looked absolutely right and natural when carried out in wood and installed. Once the staircase was in, we really felt we had a house.

Sitting in the car waiting to go back to the Dolaucothi one night – Ralph had gone in for some final word – I saw the young moon rising over the house. Quite suddenly I thought of it as a home; for the first time it belonged to me. All the nights to come when I should not be leaving; I should cook here, that bare space would become my familiar kitchen; I should sleep in that bedroom, and open my eyes to the curve of that hill and the pattern of those trees outside the window; I should sit by the fire; walk out down the ride on summer nights. For so many years the house had been empty when the moon lit it, now it had company again.

Jennifer had had a second child, a son called Gethin. One day a curious character had walked up through our new plantation below her house (he lived on the far side) and spent the afternoon sitting on the edge of our young trees, in the shadow of a hedge, watching. Jennifer is a very un-nervous person, but the silent watcher bothered her a little, having the two small children and knowing the man had once been in trouble. She mentioned it to Ivor when he came home, and he brought her another dog, called Tammy, though a bitch. She was a large, beautiful pale gold Alsatian, already larger than Dinah, and she would grow twice as big. Dinah would have to fight to retain her ascendancy as top-dog of the house. She would, too. Dinah had become a very positive character, unshakeably sweet-tempered but establishing definite rules for her own free life. She would never allow any other dog to bark at us. If Tammy, or a pretty little fluffy sheepdog Jennifer had for a time before passing it on, followed her in challenging the car, or barked and came towards us when we went on foot to visit Jennifer, Dinah turned on them fiercely and drove them back with a sharp reprimand which was always obeyed. She knew her duty as watchdog of the house, but we were her old friends, and she wouldn't let these upstarts be rude to us. Then she would come up to us with her writhing sheepdog approach, for a good pat-and-stroke of her close Alsatian coat, and a little conversation. When our building had started, we'd been afraid the unaccustomed volume of transport passing Panteg might endanger Dinah. 'I think she'll manage,' Jennifer said. 'She's very sensible.'

We realised that some of the furniture we'd been saving, in the hope of building a hide-out in our Welsh woods some day, would be better inside the house before the inner door-frames were put in. Also, it would be wise to have the men working there to help us unload. Ralph thought it would be boring to hire removal men and guide them down, so he hired a splendid van with its name, Leogem, painted in big letters on the sides, to drive himself.

He parked it in our Suffolk drive, and experienced hands helped us pack it. A Knole settee, two wing chairs, a Victorian chest of drawers which had been made by an eccentric uncle of Ralph's; these mammoths were carefully positioned among a mass of smaller things, tables and chairs, books and bookcases, rugs, pictures, mirrors, cushions, boxes of china, boxes of saucepans, and finally a six-foot steel lamp of ancient and intricate design, which we thought might look right there, though in fact we have never used it.

We set out in Leogem on a night of furious storm. I looked back at our tall willows lashing right over, and wondered if they could survive. We drove to London slowly against a 60 knot head wind. But the next morning, having infiltrated two divans into spaces carefully left for them, we drove across England in clear sunshine and moderate wind. The familiar route was full of surprises seen from the height of Leogem's cab. We stopped for breakfast at our usual charming picnic site, set in trees beside a stream, a few miles on the Welsh side of the Severn Bridge. We had to take the lamp out to get at our picnic hamper, and as it was very heavy left it standing there. I laid breakfast on the wooden table provided by the Forestry Commission, and we sat on the bench beside it. There was never anyone else there at our early hour, but passing motorists glanced curiously at us eating ham and eggs under the big lamp in the sunshine in such a rural place. At garages – buying lorry-drivers' diesel instead of petrol – we got into conversation with different people, were free of a different world, driving Leogem.

Even our own deep leafy approach road looked different from high up. As we passed Panteg Farm, Dinah rushed out barking, and was astonished to discover it was us in such unfamiliar transport. At Gilfachwen the men helped us unload and pack everything into the downstairs room which would be our spare bedroom. They had got the door in and put a lock on it, so we could store things safely – the first completed room! The settee and wing chairs we had to leave in the Big Room (as we already called the interior of the original farmhouse). I pinned dust sheets round them meticulously, but I couldn't bear to think how much dust there would be from the building of the central fireplace alone. They had been taken in through the ten-feet by ten south window embrasure, which looked rather like the great open portals of Thebes, as Pilkington's glass hadn't arrived yet. Harold Metcalfe had ruled that stone buttresses were necessary to strengthen the south and west walls. At first we had regretted this, but now they were built they gave it the tough, solid character of a border keep. The old stones used for the buttresses were indistinguishable from the stones in the walls.

Eirig was sitting on the staircase, moving down a step at a time as he sandpapered to shining smoothness the little shield-shaped pieces of wood which joined each banister to its step.

I had talked urgently to Francis Jones on the matter of cleaning. 'I'm sure you'll leave it nice and clean, but still ...?'

'I'll ask a very sweet lady, I think she'll do it for you. She's my secretary,' and here she was, dainty and distressed, standing in a flowered overall and rubber gloves holding the hose of a Hoover. 'It's no good,' she said, as Morgan pushed a barrow past her and Eirig's fine dust flew down, and someone else was smoothing a filler into the wooden roof. 'As soon as I clean anywhere they come and make it dirty again. I started upstairs, but now they've gone up there to do something to the windows, and they've got mud and plaster on their boots. Won't you let me come up here again when they've really finished, after they've gone? Then I can do a proper job.' This was our first meeting with Jean Everill. Married to an Australian badly injured in the Korean war, they lived just opposite Francis Jones.

When we drove Leogem, very light and bouncy now it was empty, to the Dolaucothi which had been our Welsh home for so long, we felt strangely divided, leaving our possessions in Gilfachwen.

The next day, 'You can move in at Christmas,' Francis Jones said with an air of triumph. 'How's that?'

Well ...! It was an idea. Gilfach' was the new thing in our lives, it would be nice to celebrate it by waking up there for the first time on Christmas morning. We would!

The boot of our car has swallowed many loads that had looked impossible when collected and waiting, but it's never looked as it did that Christmas. Yiwara is used to sharing the back seat with luggage; everything else went in the boot. Ralph arranged a careful jigsaw, culminating in the large and beautiful log basket (a Christmas and housewarming present from Mrs Anderson, our Scots secretary for twenty years, and her family) which he filled with Christmas fare – a turkey, pudding, cake, mince pies – and padded it all around its base with oranges, nuts, and all the things from our garden; sprouts, cabbages, lettuces, a string of onions, a big box of apples, another of potatoes, chicory, celery. A box of Christmas presents, ours to open, and those to give. Yiwara's food, a box of meat and one of rusks, both large – she's a large dog.

Then there were plants, shrubs, herbs, carefully packed and labelled, which we hoped to establish there. Verena and Reg, the sister and brother who have looked after our house and garden for so long – looked after us and our dogs too, and who are so much a part of our lives – helped us prepare for Wales as they had over so many years helped us prepare for sailing. Indeed, setting out for Gilfachwen had much in common with setting off for *Mary Deare*. There was the same feeling of being self-dependent and cut off, of creating a complete way of life.

The night of the 23rd we spent at the Dolaucothi. After unpacking and attempting to distribute things at Gilfach', how glorious to go back and sleep in a bed one hadn't made, bath without considering whether the water was hot – or indeed whether it actually flowed into the house at all – to eat a meal one hadn't planned, bought, cooked, would clear up.

On Christmas Eve we left the Dolaucothi, never to sleep there again, though often to dine.

We set the car's head up into the mountains, turned down our own road now winter-bare, yet vivid with emerald grass, rust-red bracken and creamy drifts of Molinia grass and spangled with berries; past Panteg with Gethin and Gwyneth standing on their garden wall waving (no Dinah?), and arrived at Gilfachwen with a sense of climacteric to take up residence.

'First things first,' said Ralph, 'Sit down.'

I unpinned the dust sheets without daring to pat the furniture to see how much dust was in it, and sat down. Diana Cooley had given us an exquisite plate as a Christmas and housewarming present, and I put it in the middle of my mother's carved Indian table which was also starting a new life, bridging the generations and the continents.

Ralph opened a bottle of Krug, and we toasted the new life of the house, and our life there.

After sharing the bottle of champagne we felt much stronger, which was fortunate, as the heating, which had made the place superbly warm on our last visit, when the men were still here, didn't appear to be working and it was very cold, the damp of new walls, and of old walls recently pointed-up, drying out gradually. Jennifer had put on the electricity, and adjusted the thermostats two days before, but nothing seemed to be happening. Ralph thought there might be a speck of dust blocking the thermostats, so he blew and patted and twiddled.

I started on the house. I'd had my hair done for Christmas (to impress the sheep?) but having had it done I wanted to keep it nice, so I put first a scarf then a shower cap over it. The result was so very unbecoming that a glance in a mirror did nothing for my morale – who was this drudge? Then I started on the house. Dear Jean Everill's efforts had made it just possible, but the men had indeed followed her up. Ralph had assembled an Electrolux and was cleaning.

I hadn't yet got shelves in the kitchen, or a dresser in the Big Room for my beautiful eighteenth-century blue and white floral dinner service, so I put all the china for safety in the bottom of two kitchen cupboards. As I had recently injured my knee and couldn't kneel, this was awkward. Stores couldn't be put in the cupboards till I'd swept out the debris of plaster, cigarette ends, dead flies, then washed them. The fridge was working perfectly – I'd put the turkey, dog's meat, eggs, butter, milk, cheeses, bacon, etc. in yesterday. Ralph had checked the cooker by switching on the grill, which worked, but when I tried the oven, it didn't. As always in moments of disaster, my mind flashed to Plan B: – carve turkey raw and grill in sections if no oven, eat in kitchen if no heat in Big Room.

But whatever Ralph had done to the thermostats was what they liked. The heat came on, gradually permeating the house with comfort. He spoke to the oven and that worked too – no need for Plan B. I made up the beds, spreading at last the beautiful *carthan* (Welsh hand-woven bedspread) in powder blue and pale gold, bought on a visit to St David's when the house was still a dream, and which had dictated the colour scheme of the bedroom; hung the blue chintz curtains, put up the flame-silk lampshades I had made; cleaned the wardrobe and hung up our clothes; put the big blue tapestry cushion in my mother's old bentwood rocking chair. Ralph hung the pictures, and some mirrors we had put in Victorian frames. By evening the house was becoming almost human. Soup and a cold supper in the kitchen, this was no time for cooking. I had cleaned the new bath, the water was boiling hot and flowed powerfully; very soft water from a mountain spring. Utter sleep in the new beds.

I woke on Christmas morning to see the small north window exactly framing that perfect beech tree, as I had known it would. The big south window framed the frieze of apple, cherry, laburnum and ash that fringed the little garden, and beyond them the hillsides always patched with the pale blurs of sheep, and Jennifer's ponies in the nearer field.

Coming downstairs, the warm tiles were delicious to bare feet; I found Yiwara had got up from her rug at the foot of the stairs and was standing in front of the big window staring fascinated at the ponies and sheep so close, (we had set the fence about twelve feet away on this side, as the hill fell steeply).

Christmas breakfast was the first meal cooked here, and I felt, as I had done on *Mary Deare*, the strange sense of playing a game when using all the equipment so carefully planned, and finding it actually worked. Breakfast was and remained a kitchen meal, with the teak table and chairs I had given Ralph for his birthday – for the garden! but they looked so nice in the kitchen we left them there.

Playing house absorbed me. Ralph put in the plants we had brought from the garden at home. I put red candles in candlesticks brought from all over the world, coming into their own in this setting, and found some evergreens. We opened our Christmas cards over a drink before lunch, and I hung them on long red ribbons along the stockade-like staircase. Ralph was bringing in logs for the fire – very important.

We dined in state in the Big Room, first meal there Christmas dinner. Ralph got the fire going in the spectacular fire basket Harold Metcalfe had designed and Garnet Rees had made. Owing to some breakdown in communication between Metcalfe's office and Francis Jones, the curtain rods so carefully discussed way back had not materialised. My huge curtains remained in bundles collecting creases, and the black night looked in through the south wall of glass, the patio door at the back, and the four deep original windows in the front. Yet, strangely, this was not menacing or cheerless; partly because the room was warm, also because of the lighting which, concealed, ran all round the room where the vertical stone walls met the sloping wood above. Harold Metcalfe's first lighting plan of stage-set glamour, we had rejected as being far too expensive. 'Never mind!' he'd said cheerfully, 'Here's another idea. It'll cost much less, and look very nice.'

It would have an imperceptible tint. 'I hate coloured lighting,' I had snapped when he suggested it. 'Of course you do, so do I,' he had answered imperturbably. 'You won't see any colour. It will just look pleasant, instead of cold and white and hard.' It was one of his inspirations. You couldn't define any colour, but it somehow gave the effect of early spring sunshine. Flooding down over the pearly grey stones, emphasising their contours, picking out every irregular surface and the soft

shadows between – I felt we were sitting out in some southern courtyard.

Ralph set a bottle of Charmes Chambertin a carefully-judged distance from the fire. This was part of Alfred Knopf's Christmas present; he had been Ralph's American publisher until his retirement, and we still kept in touch. I cooked a twelve-pound turkey in that little oven; Verena had stuffed it with her two beautiful stuffings, and sewn it up neatly. One of her usual delectable puddings, rich but light, completed its boiling. I had made brandy butter at home, only vegetables and bread sauce to worrry about on the night.

We didn't want TV or a phone here, so Ralph had bought a very fine record player and radio equipment and installed it in the still unfurnished room at the top of the stairs; sound flowed down through the three long, two-foot deep slits in the wall. I put a tall candle in each of these; it was like looking up to a minstrels' gallery.

Firelight and candlelight, wine and music and feasting; Gilfachwen had really come to life again.

The next day we walked down to Panteg to greet the Thomases, but they were all out. Dinah crawled to meet us, looking awful – ragged coat and hollow sides. I didn't yet know Jennifer very well, but even then it seemed unthinkable Dinah was neglected. When we were driving out and saw they were at home, we stopped to chat. 'What's the matter with Dinah?' I asked. 'Come and look in the barn and you'll see!' Jennifer said, leading the way, and there was a litter of beautiful puppies. Dinah, an assumed eight years old at least, had produced for the first time. 'She's one of those dogs who don't show when she's on heat. I did notice a rather nice black dog from a farm on the other side of the forestry came about the place, but I didn't think anything of it. I didn't know until just the other day. I thought she was getting fat and examined her. She had some difficulty as it was her first litter rather late in life. I came down in the night to see how she was getting on, and had to help her with the last one.'

Jennifer distracted Dinah with a bowl of milk and showed us

the puppies. Tammy danced around fascinated, but Dinah snarled her off from the nest. 'Sometimes she lets Tammy come up and sniff them,' Jennifer said. Though quarter-bred, they had the character of Alsatian puppies, tough and bumbly, already seeking the face of anyone holding them, to look into their eyes and find out what they were like.

That was the year of the great storm on January 2, the storm that swept a swathe of destruction across England. It came from our exposed corner, the south-west. 'Useful to see what it can do to us,' Ralph said. 'This will find any weak spots.'

The main violence of the storm passed over us; (who had said, 'they knew where to build, the old people!') But torrential rain forced against the house by wind gusting over 100 mph found every minute crevice in the cement between the stone walls and the aluminium window-frames. Gradually one, two, three, four little streams crept from each of the deep window sills and slid down the walls to meander across the floor. We moved the rugs, the tiles would take no harm.

'Shall we eat in the kitchen?' Ralph suggested, thinking it would save trouble; we were leaving in the morning. I felt that would be rather a come-down. I loved the glamour of the Big Room at night. 'Oh no! Let's have one more lovely evening.'

So we dined as usual; eating something very simple, probably pasta with a nice sauce, and the last of our mince pies, nuts and fruit from Christmas; sometimes even the two-foot thick stone walls shook in the violence of the storm, while the four little rivulets advanced slowly across the floor – quite in character for a southern courtyard; the room was still warm and sunny-looking. Suddenly headlights swept a swathe of light through the uncurtained windows.

'Someone's come,' I said. 'A car's arrived.'

'Don't be ridiculous.' Ralph was sitting with his back to the window. 'Do you really think anyone would come out here on a night like this?' Then we heard the knock on the door.

It was Francis Jones. He'd been driving home along the main road, and had decided to turn off and come to see how we were – how the house he had built was standing up to this! A mile and a half extra, here and back, on a rough road running with water, the gale beating on the car. A visit to remember!

He sat down and had a whisky. 'Isn't that what they call a silk Kashan?' this astonishing man asked, looking at an old rug we had hung on the wall. How did he know? I remember we discussed Port Moresby in Papua New Guinea, which he had visited during the war when he was in the Merchant Navy. It was strangely tranquil in the old stone house, while the storm banged over our heads against the hill behind us, and the little waterfalls fell from the window sills down the glistening stones, and moved over the tiles.

He pinpointed the source of the leaks, and would seal them in our absence – we had asked him to keep a key. Before we left the next day, Ralph labelled each point where water had entered, and there was no more trouble. And before our next visit, Jean Everill came up and cleaned Gilfach'. Her husband drove her up, and held the ladder while she cleaned the high windows, which she insisted on doing. They didn't just clean the house, they polished and cherished it. Everything shone, furniture, glass, floors. 'Now we've got it clean from its building, I think it's a house that will keep clean pretty well,' she said. 'I don't think there'll be much work,' and this proved true.

Visits fell into a pattern of seasons. Blackthorn time, foaming like snow, and the woods full of wild cherry. Early summer, when the hawthorn hedges across England are creamy-white, and in our corner of Wales the laburnums are in bloom. This is a glory I have never heard of or read about, it seems a secret, local miracle. A forester who heard me describe them as 'wild' corrected me, saying, 'They are not literally a wild species, they must be wind-borne or bird-carried, or both.' Presumably something in the soil is exactly right, because every hedge is patched with groups of laburnums – not small pale flowers either, but long, heavy rich yellow racemes, like the Vossii variety grown in gardens. At first I imagined it had survived where once there had been a garden, but no. This theory quickly became absurd because they were everywhere. The whole countryside is lit with golden trees. There is a field

182

near one of our plantations whose four hedges are all laburnum. Driving about this small area at this season – never to be missed – one is in a perpetual exclamation, 'Look! Look! the laburnums!' Every lane, and the high wild hillsides are yellow with the sunshine of laburnums. There are bluebells in the hedges too, and the massed ferns are uncurling their fronds while you watch, and the whole green countryside is bleating with lambs. A pair of buzzards nest in one of our big beech trees just below the house, and their mewing cry is constant as they swoop and plane back and forth to feed their young.

I was desperate to find a dresser to get my dinner service on to, and out of the kitchen cupboard. The most dreary and dubious pieces were described as 'Welsh Dressers' and offered for ludicrous prices at local sales. Diana Cooley kept a watching brief for us, and one evening when we had gone to the Dolaucothi for dinner (Diana was a Cordon Bleu cook), Glen Cooley said to us over the bar, 'I believe the Everills have got a dresser they don't want. He was in here the other night and said they hadn't room for it and had put it in the barn. I've no idea what it's like.'

It was only about 9.30 when we left the Dolaucothi – was it too late to visit the Everills on the way home? Perhaps not, on a lovely spring night with a moon, and a dresser in prospect. So we turned down the road where we had first gone to visit Francis Jones. They were the only two houses in this deep, narrow lane. Rex Everill must have heard the car, or the latch of his garden gate, he was at the door almost as we knocked.

'Come and look,' he said. Jean was going to bed because they were setting off somewhere early the next morning. She came out in a flowered housecoat, looking very pretty. We all walked through the garden to the barn. The dresser was almost buried in straw. 'Let's get it out,' Rex said. He pushed off the straw, and as it was dark in the barn, he and Ralph lifted it out into the moonlight. It was charming. Not antique, about fifty years or so, a well-made piece by a good carpenter. Ralph remembered the measurements we wanted, and they were perfect. It was what would have been known as a 'cottage display cabinet'.

They promised to get Francis Jones to bring it out in two days' time, and wouldn't hear of our deciding until we'd seen it in position. So we tucked it back into the straw.

They all came out with it. Jean wanted to see a mare of hers Jennifer was looking after, she was in the field behind Gilfach'. It must have been one of Rex Everill's better days, because I remember him fairly leaping down the steep bank after visiting the horse, waving his crutches in the air. He was a powerfully built man, and for that evening was on top of his encroaching injuries. He insisted on helping Ralph and Francis Jones take the dresser from the van and carry it into the house. One felt he would have liked to pick it up by himself, leaving his crutches against the wall.

Standing under the three interior windows, between the front door and the kitchen door, balancing the big south window at the far end, it looked at home, exactly right. I couldn't wait to arrange my dinner service on it. They asked such a small sum that Ralph insisted on paying more, thinking what it could have made if they'd put it in a sale.

Nothing daunted, when we next visited them, Jean gave me a charming print of a water colour by Birket Foster. With the special firmness of very gentle people, she told me where to hang it. 'I think it would look nice in the downstairs cloakroom, the wall to the left of the door.' I doubted if this was worthy of it, though I loved the superb stonework there, and the porthole window. But having tried it everywhere else, I realised she was quite right – in full light, on the primrose wall beside the stone wall, near enough to look at closely. So there it hangs.

It had worried us, when we came down during the building, that we could never offer the men a drink at the end of the day. 'We'll have a Housewarming!' we'd said. Just for the people who had worked on the house, and our foresters, as that was the reason for our being there.

It was the following November before we could arrange this. Francis Jones came to fix the shelves he had made for the kitchen, then he sat down over a cup of coffee and gave me the addresses of all the men, and the names of their wives and girl friends, and I sent invitation cards. We asked Diana Cooley to look after the food, as she did such lovely cold tables, and we would bring the drinks.

I still have all the answering letters. We were about thirty. I picked branches of coloured leaves and berries and put them in big pitchers. Candles everywhere of course. Diana brought a long trestle table, and I had brought from home a huge old white damask cloth which we pinned round it, and her spread of dishes looked marvellous. Her two helpers took over the kitchen. Ralph set out whisky and wine and beer; he would be barman. He had made out a big notice saying: *Croeso! Dewch mewn!* ('Welcome! Please walk in!' in Welsh), and pinned it on the front door. We switched on all the lights, outside as well as in, to beacon them along the road.

We knew the men, but not their wives. The girls came in long dresses, several of them really beautiful, many bringing flowers. Harold Metcalfe brought a flashlight camera, but was too busy talking to use it. I would dearly have loved a picture of that room full of the men who had built it. They talked in Welsh of course, but when either of us joined a group they switched with instant Celtic courtesy to English. Francis Jones had asked whether to wear a dinner jacket; I'd told him Ralph hadn't got one with him, so he came in an exquisite shirt, take him to the Savoy any time. Ivor Thomas, usually so silent (and looking very handsome) was having a serious political conversation with Harold Metcalfe, the electrician, and our forester Cyrus Williams.

Garnet Rees, the powerful blacksmith (I'd never seen him other than in working clothes before; the standard of looks was high at this party) prowled around the fireplace he had built, worrying because it smoked unless constantly tended. I noticed later that he'd got Harold Metcalfe on to this too. Garnet lay full length on the floor, the better to look up the chimney; he was a tall man, and went on a long way.

I remember Jennifer sitting on a low stool in the middle of the room, for that one moment alone and silent, as if her thoughts were far away. She'd come in a beautiful long black dress that

swept round her, with her black curls and brilliant colouring she looked like a gypsy queen – an almost theatrical centrepiece to the noisy, animated room.

We were interested that so many of them drank wine. Morgan Lewis drank whisky, to give him strength for that wheelbarrow, perhaps. Every time I passed his little group he said, 'Missus! Can I have some more whisky?' I thought this was rather rude at first and ignored it, until I noticed he said it even when his glass was nearly full, and I realised it was a joke. Later in the evening he changed it to 'Missus! Are we going to have a party every week?' He did enjoy whisky, but he seemed no different at the end of the evening from the beginning. We did ascertain that he was not driving himself home.

After supper Ralph made a little speech, explaining that everyone there had contributed to the house in some way; 'Even my wife. She made the curtains, and as you see, there's a lot of them.' (Alternate widths of pale silvery green and regency red, I was pleased with them now they were up at last.)

We had wondered in advance how this party would ever end. It was Friday night, no one was going to work tomorrow, there seemed no reason why they should ever go. In fact, I had glanced at the possibility of having a few for the night. But

Harold Metcalfe made a charming speech thanking us, and this in a way said goodbye – he and his wife had a long way to go back to Carmarthen, it was nice of them to come so far. But I had underestimated the perfect manners of our guests, everyone left in perfect order, and there were no accidents on the wild road home. Didn't someone say all the Welsh are descended from princes?

Two guests I was sad to miss. John and Blodwyn Williams, who had come to visit us one day, had known Gilfach' in its previous existence, had even been to a party here! They were my one direct link with the past, and I had wanted them to bridge the two parties. But on the evening Blodwyn had a cold, so their son brought a note of apology and a housewarming present John had made himself; a wooden hat-hanger with the name and date carved on it. They were the people who could tell me about the house, about who had lived here, and about that other tumbledown house between us and Panteg, which had such a strong character that one almost hesitated to duck under the big trees and sit on its broken walls. I must get them here on their own, and ask questions.

There seemed perpetual entertainment to be seen through the windows of Gilfach'. An effect I loved was the strange metamorphosis of the view seen, as in four picture frames, through the deep square windows facing west. With the sun setting in various colours and mists, the country seemed to stretch away into endless ranges, bearing no relation to the familiar daytime country. I thought of it as the hills of Colorado (a place I have never seen). This happened just at the time when, dinner prepared and cooking, I sat down for a drink, and I regarded it as an important engagement, not to be missed. At last I thought of trying to relate this mysterious land with the view – beautiful but quite different – by day, and realised that alternate streaks of dark trees and pale fields gave this impression of range upon range when the mists of sunset blurred them.

Once, watching this, Ralph said very quietly, 'Look to your left. Don't move.' Yiwara had twitched her ears and her eyes were focussed through the big south window. The field was in shadow after the dazzling west. Something was moving; a fox, wandering at ease up the hillside through the long summer grasses; and something else behind him, another fox, and together, romping, they made their leisurely way to the top of the hill.

Yiwara reacted more strongly to the white cat. This was a large, powerful, predatory cat who hunted alone. I think she had taken to the wild, and was so used to Gilfach' being empty that she rather resented our intrusion. She (or he) had a particularly malevolent expression, partly due to the slant of a black streak above one eye. From time to time we saw her slipping through the forestry, very plump, the hunting was good.

She was not the only one who resented us. The rooks, whose colony had been such a feature of the house when a ruin, did not easily relinquish it. We arrived once to find several windows apparently streaked with blood; the rooks had been gorging on elderberries and then attacking the house! There was a pattern of claw marks on the glass, and long white scratches where they had swiped with their beaks. Yiwara called us at first light, to warn us the rooks were attacking. Ralph was startled to find her pawing him as she was not supposed to come upstairs (the staircase, being open at the back, was dangerous for a big dog on the downward journey, but she realised this and was careful). 'Ah, it's their house,' Francis Jones said, 'It's been their house for a long time, many generations.'

But how did they know? Inherited memory? They gave up gradually, but in our absence ate out all the putty round the window frames, because they liked the linseed oil it contained. We had to have them redone with a material not containing linseed.

Jennifer sometimes had ponies, sometimes heifers in the fields behind the house, and always the trespassing sheep, coming from the farmer over the hill, so the passage of neighbour animals was part of our day – sweeping up from south to north every morning, down again from north to south every evening through the whole stretch of the communicating fields. Coming down in the morning, one sometimes startled a huge flight of magpies, who swooped off down the field in a black and white cloud looking enormous, like penguins.

Gwyneth and Gethin were shooting up. Visiting Jennifer one day, I saw something new in her sitting-room; a very pretty Victorian piano, charmingly painted, with beautiful brass candlesticks on either side. 'I bought it in a sale at Lampeter,' she said. 'I hadn't meant to, but I got it for £3! It's a good one, I had the music teacher try it, and she said it only needed tuning, so I'm getting that done. I think Gwyneth will be musical, she shows signs of it, so I thought it would be nice for her to be able to practise at home when she's old enough to take lessons.'

Dinah had bounced back into condition after her litter, and again leaped down from the wall, scorning the steps. Tammy was full grown, very handsome, blonde, with strange pale eyes. She was generally in the barn, an unfailing house dog with a good deep bark – the Panteg dogs always warned Yiwara when anything was coming down our road – but I thought that if she were out, and Dinah was not about to look after me, I might be a little bit doubtful of Tammy.

Then once again Dinah came slowly down the steep steps, greeted us affectionately, but kept turning her head to show us a deep hole in her shoulder.

'She had a terrible fight with Tammy,' Jennifer told us. 'It was a final sort of fight, to the death. The children were involved, they were all playing together. Both dogs were absolutely gentle with the children, but they turned on each other, I think probably one got jealous because she thought the children were paying more attention to the other, but basically it was because Tammy was challenging to become top dog, and Dinah's always been top dog and she wouldn't give in. But she's older, and only half Tammy's size. I couldn't separate them, so I ran for the first thing I could find, which was Gethin's little chair! I went for Tammy with that and drove her off and got Dinah away. I had to. Tammy meant to kill her.'

Jennifer sounded almost apologetic, as though I might think she'd been hard on Tammy. On the contrary, I thought she'd been heroic – I wouldn't have cared to go for Tammy with a child's chair!

Yet the two dogs came to terms and tolerated each other again, sometimes even played together. Tammy and Gethin used to romp together, rolling over and over, the big paws wrapped gently round the little boy. I remember a procession strung out like a Greek frieze, walking across the hill field; Jennifer in a long cloak that streamed in the breeze, carrying a bucket of feed to a pony, followed by Gwyneth, Gethin, Dinah, Tammy, a pet lamb they had at that time, and a ginger cat.

We went to an Eisteddfod in Pumpsaint; the road was lined with cars far out from the village. Choirs had come from far and wide, each bringing their supporters. There was a women's choir, and one of the men's choirs had a woman conductor. Most of the numbers were original works, written for this event, sung in Welsh, of course. The village hall was packed, but some people kindly closed up to make room for us on a bench beside the wall. The hall was very hot and the lights glaring – we went out into the road to cool off in the interval – but we went back for the second half, it was too exciting to miss. We didn't stay till the end, I heard it went on till morning!

I found out where John and Blodwyn Williams lived, and asked them to come and spend an evening with us. I had been quite wrong in my impression of them when they had come unexpectedly to see us. Perhaps because they came up over the hill at evening, I had an impression of a small, almost gnome-like couple who might have risen out of the ground from some legend. But when I visited them in their nice modern house on the outskirts of Lampeter to fix a date, I found John was tall, and Blodwyn about my height.

They came and sat by our fire, with drinks settled comfortably beside them, and their lilting Welsh voices flowed on through the evening, alternating and overlapping each other, supplementing each other's memories, drawing the past around us. It's they who belonged here, we who were the visitors.

The most recent history we knew. The previous owner, from whom we had bought the land and the three houses, had lived in Panteg and used Gilfachwen for storing hay and feeding stuffs. His wife (who was said to have thrown the clock at him out of the window) was 'spoken of as having joined him from a Fair – something to do with show business they did say'. They confirmed he had worked desperately to farm the land, and indeed we had seen all the drainage he had put in by himself, by hand; but he had lacked the capital to make it pay, and had to sell.

'And the middle house, Ystafellwen? (pronounced *Estavidwen*), meaning "the white chamber"' I asked.

'Ah, he didn't use that,' John said. 'No one's lived there since Mrs Ann Lewis.'

'I've heard of her from Francis Jones,' I told them. 'He speaks of her as a very remarkable old lady. Says she had a pony and trap, bought vegetables from the farmers and took them round to the miners – went all over the country. And she was the midwife for this area.'

'She wasn't always an old lady!' Blodwyn laughed. 'When she first came to Ystafellwen she was a young girl – she came as a bride! Her husband worked down the mine.'

'Everyone did,' John explained. 'If they were lucky, there was nothing else. But you had to have influence to get down the mine, there were so many after every job. But he was lucky, he'd got a job, he'd been down the mine since he was fourteen, that was the usual thing. They had five or six children. But they had some bad luck, he got ill, you see ...' John Williams coughed, 'The lungs, you know, what's the name?'

'Silicosis,' Blodwyn whispered, 'Very bad, very usual in those days. So after a while he couldn't go to work, he sat at home.'

'How did they live?'

'She knitted stockings!' John cut in. 'She'd beg a fleece from a rich farmer, and she'd persuade the factory at Cellan to spin it for her, and she'd knit those long thick woollen stockings! All the time she knitted, always she was knitting stockings! It was endless, those stockings! Then she'd walk over the mountains to sell them at Brynamuran Fair. This was what they lived on chiefly.'

'It seems quite a big house. Were there outbuildings?'

'Yes. They had a pig, sometimes a farmer would give them a pig, and they'd keep it all the year. Then later she had a little shop there.'

'A shop?' Ralph asked. 'Who was there to buy?'

'Yes, a shop, for the scattered farms in the hills. She'd fetch sugar, and flour, and yeast, in her pony and trap – a very small pony it was – and that helped the people who'd no way of going to town.'

'Weren't they lonely, so cut off?' I pondered, 'She and her family?'

'No, they were not lonely. There were people here at Gilfachwen, and people at Panteg. They were a little community, you see, these three farms. Then the postman came.'

'Did she have post?'

'Sometimes she might have post, from her relations maybe, and the postman passed along your road here on his way back from going round to the farms, you see. It was a long rough round for him over the mountains, so always she had a bowl of soup for him!'

'Yes!' Blodwyn said, 'Every single day – she knew what time he'd come, and have his bowl of soup ready. She grew vegetables, and there was the pig, and she grew herbs for flavouring. She had a peat fire – you can see on the mountain where she cut the peat. It was one of those fireplaces with bars to balance the pots, and the oven at the side, and the heat was under the oven – the same as they had here,' She pointed to where our fire was now.

'What did her husband do?'

'He wrote! Yes! He'd got some education, I don't quite know how that happened, and he wrote all the time. There was a row once when Annie in a hurry wrapped some sugar up in one of the pages of his manuscript. He was very intelligent. He gradually collected all the history and legend of this area. I never read it, only a very few of his friends read his manuscript, but they said it was wonderful what he'd found out.'

'There's a lot to find out, round here,' Ralph said as he got up to re-fill glasses and put logs on the fire. 'What about that great conglomerate stone on the hill just behind us, by the Sarn Helen?'*

'Ah, no one knows about that – how it got here – but they do say it's one of the oldest things in Britain. But what there is to know, the ideas people have handed down – he'd found out, and written it, so it should be kept, you see. Craig Twrch, that's the name of the hill ... They say he'd made a marvellous record of everything round here, going right back ... Extraordinary things he'd found, just by asking, and talking to people.'

'She kept it after his death,' Blodwyn said. 'I don't know if she could read or not, but she knew it was something important, because of all the work he'd put into it; years of work. Just a candle they had in the evening, if they could afford it. She had a little girl to live with her for company after he died, but she left when she was twelve, to go and work at a farm – it was the usual thing.'

'So she was alone then?'

'Yes,' Blodwyn answered. 'And when she died, and her children came to clear the place up and get her things, they burnt all the papers, all his manuscript.'

'Just pieces of paper,' John said. 'It's a sad loss. All his work. All he found out.'

'She's buried in Llancrwys churchyard,' Blodwyn said. 'You can see her grave.'

And her currant and gooseberry bushes are still fruiting under the great trees that now screen the tumbled walls of her house. Ralph has retrieved a patch of her garden from the nettles and planted some herbs and seedling shrubs. Ystafellwen had always had a very strong presence to me – not hostile, just still occupied.

John Williams had also gone down the mine at fourteen. 'Yes, I was lucky, I got a job.' He had actually worked in Ogofau, the gold mine at Pumpsaint. This mine was thought to be one of the chief reasons why the Romans invaded Britain. They built

* The Roman road.

seven miles of sluices, and exported 400 tons of gold a year back to Rome.

It continued to be worked in a small way up to the 1930s, when the workings had moved so far underground, and the world price of gold was so low, that it was no longer economic. (Now, with modern machinery, and the world price of gold high, there is talk of re-opening Ogofau.)

The whole area of the old workings is now grown over with grass and trees, but they don't grow quite right; a strange, steep, higgledy-piggledy place, rather creepy, and you need a torch at night if you're not to fall down old mine shafts, and keep your dog on a lead. It had been one of our after-dinner dog walks during the years we used to stay at the Dolaucothi. One day archaeologists suddenly dug up the car park of the Dolaucothi, and found the old Roman guard post from which the mine had been controlled. Having recorded it, they covered it all up again, so we still park on top of it.

And John had actually worked down Ogofau as a boy! 'Yes, it was strange, you know, those old workings, we were through to the passages the Romans had worked, no one had been there since, it gave you a funny feeling. Sometimes we would break through to a chamber which had been sealed (by a fall) ever since they left. It would be full of water, and the water would come gushing out through the hole we had made, and the smell ...! The smell of stagnant water which had been collecting all those years, all those hundreds of years. It was something terrible, I can tell you! Awful! We would all run and run, as fast and as far as we could, to get away from it, to get out, and breathe the good air again. The water was up to our armpits, you see. The water had force – we'd broken into an old shaft, and there was the weight of two or three hundred feet of water behind it.'

The party Blodwyn remembered at Gilfach' had been a birthday party. 'Yes, I seem to remember it was a good party!' she said, 'Everyone talking and laughing, and something nice to eat. She had blue china on her dresser like you have!' (I found a broken bit in the garden.) 'And they had a very nice grandfather clock, but it was too tall for the room – the ceiling was right down when there was an upstairs above this, you see. So they made a hole in the floor and dug down to bury the bottom of it, so it was looking at you quite close, that big face. That's where it stood, just there.'

'But I don't understand how the house could fall to pieces so badly in the time?' I said.

She leant forward in her chair and spoke confidentially, with sudden emphasis, 'It was falling to pieces already, before they left! Those were hard times here in Wales, they were the bad years; there was no money for repairs, no money for anything.'

Evans had been their name, Rachel and John Evans, and Blodwyn told me where to find their son, Tommy Evans, who had been born here, and perhaps he could tell me who had lived here before them, and before that . . . Someday I would go and find him.

Early in the year Dinah had another litter, quite easily this

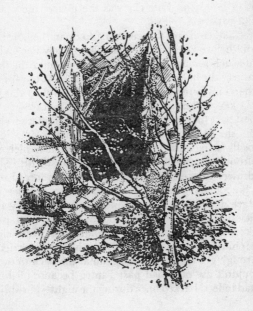

time, and made her nest so deep in the wall opposite Panteg that Jennifer had to put the whole length of her arm in to fetch the puppies out; it was cold wet weather and she thought they'd all be better in the barn where she could keep an eye on them. Again, they were lovely puppies, looking like true Alsatians, solid and bumbly and determined, turning their funny little round heads about to search for your face, as soon as their own eyes were open.

Tammy was no more. She had gone for the pet lamb and chased a sheep. This is death for a dog in that country.

Then one leisurely day of full summer we arrived later than usual, and as luck would have it, we came into Wales by a different route so we didn't pass the Dolaucothi, where there was a message for us. We approached Gilfachwen un-warned, and saw two cars, and Jennifer talking to several men. With great succinctness she said, 'I am sorry to have to tell you that you have had a break-in.' One car was the police, the other the fingerprint expert.

Jennifer had come up that morning to clean the house as she always did before we arrived – this was entirely her own idea, and made such a marvellous welcome. She found the door on to the patio at the back badly damaged; they'd cut near the lock to get a hand in, found a kind of safety lock invulnerable except to its own key, so knocked in the bottom panel.

The best part (oddly enough not all) of my dinner service had gone from the dresser, and all the old Chinese plates from the window-sills, a modern tea-set from the kitchen shelves, one picture from upstairs, and a few unusual oddments. The one locked drawer in the chest-of-drawers upstairs forced open, a pair of binoculars gone but an enamel dressing set left. A knowledgeable china thief, knowing exactly what he wanted – and efficient. He must have brought all his own packing materials, as obvious things like newspapers, blankets, cloths to wrap the china in were not touched, they had then carried them all over rough ground up the steep hill at the back to the road. They couldn't use our road past Panteg because of the dogs. Dinah had indeed barked once during the night – possibly when they broke the glass in the door, the only noisy thing they did; she might have heard that across two fields, and her bark would have hurried them.

Jennifer, when she realised what had happened, went to the nearest phone, a callbox on the main road, about a mile from Gilfach'. It had been vandalised – it frequently is. So she set out, with Gwyneth and Gethin, as she couldn't leave them, to walk to her mother's. This is about three miles going dead straight across the tops, then down and down into the valley and across the ford (Gethin had walked to his grandmother's before, he liked walking). She telephoned the police, and asked them to pick her up at Ffarmers and bring her back with them.

Later, when Ralph thanked her for coping so well, she sighed and said, 'Yes, I think it's been the longest day of my life.'

We gathered that gossip in the pubs knew who had done it, and who his assistant had been, where they both lived, and the other five jobs they'd done. (The assistant left a packet of Slug-death on the wall, and this was traced, through a shop who had only stocked six packets of that brand, of which only one was sold to someone they didn't know. Nice sleuthing, but it didn't help.) The police knew too, but couldn't prove it. The burglar told a chum what the night's work was worth, and it was just about the same sum our insurance assessed it at (he must have had a very good fence). It seemed a very chatty burglary, one felt one might be having a drink beside the burglar in some bar at any moment, so detailed was the gossip about who had done it.

The dinner service was photographed from what was left, circulated far and wide but nothing was found. Either it was whisked out of the country through Fishguard to Ireland and thence to America (the usual route) or else it was buried. So I still glance round every antique shop.

Months would pass. From very far away it was strange to think of that lonely house in the wild mountains, holding all the familiar details of our life there. Then we would come back from the ends of the earth and turn in at our gate (we'd cleaned up the entrance and now had two nice oak gates with a stone wall on either side) and look again at the great bowl in the hills full of our own trees, always taller, and the unchanging lines of the hills beyond. Drive again down the beautiful track fringed with heather and rowan berries, or broom, or foxgloves, or cherry. As we slipped down the steep cut that opens out in front of Panteg Farm we would look for Dinah. 'Yes, there she is', a part of all our arrivals, that little grey shadow standing across the track, her head turned to face the oncoming car, guarding the pass.

The same conversations with the same people were picked up as if no other life in some strange far-away world lay between. The 'Milk' notice was now buried in the hedge, but we knew the narrow turning to Jennifer's mother's farm. The hazard of this visit was always her very small King Charles spaniel, who welcomed us, but barked at Yiwara in the car. Yiwara replied furiously, leaping about in the back, and as Ralph had to turn in a very difficult entrance (while I bought the milk), he could not at the same time stop her savaging the leather with her claws. The worst time this happened was the morning the whole family came to the door with congratulations for Ralph on his CBE. We'd thought it was coming, but had no idea when it would be announced, and apparently it had been on the radio, TV and in the morning papers. At last I tore myself away and went happily off to pass all this on to Ralph, and found our car had gone far along the lane, still pursued by the tiny barking dog (presumably full of the joys of spring, as she'd never come beyond her own gateway before). Ralph was furious, having been trying to turn the car in a rather narrow muddy gap, and at the same time restrain Yiwara from shredding the back of the car – also avoid running over the minute, invisible but incessantly barking King Charles spaniel. 'What on earth have you been doing? You've never been so long. Couldn't you hear the dogs?' By the time we got to our usual garage, to be greeted with 'Mentioned in despatches this morning, I see', he was becoming mollified.

Jennifer had acquired a very droopy basset bitch, who waddled rather pompously after Dinah, but was kept well in place by her, and later a spaniel puppy arrived. Gethin went to school now. We slipped into our life there as if we had never been away. The sheep drifting by at dawn; the hills of Colorado at sunset, the cabaret of the fields; one evening something moving in the ride in front of the house turned out through the glasses to be a very large hare taking his supper, and behind him, nearer the cover of the trees, a smaller hare, probably the doe, also eating. Then at the far end of the ride, a fox slipped across from side to side. These animals must have been aware of each other, but they gave no sign. The fox disappeared into the trees (and later came up the field beyond the house). The doe slipped into cover. The big hare continued eating for some time then, probably feeling himself observed, froze and sat like a stone; you could see him thinking with his ears.

Yiwara contributed a lot to the evenings, especially in the winter. A lonely house in wild country can be a trifle uneasy at night without a dog lying about the floor, to hear anything there is to hear before you could, so you never need to listen.

But the house was wonderfully cosy at night, and indeed these hills, peopled for so many centuries, are not unfriendly, however wild and lonely. Somehow it is not 'lonely' country. You may know there is nobody for miles, yet there is a curious sense of busy-ness, of movement just below the surface. I have often wandered some way down the road at night to look back at the lights of the house, and felt perfectly confident – but companioned.

Coming home late after dining at the Dolaucothi, we would sometimes find Dinah still out, waiting for us in her accustomed place. In the headlights her paws and underbody showed white, and her eyes glittered like lights. She might have been a ghost dog.

Sometimes she seemed to be tiring; one spring departure we left her sitting in the sunshine in front of her house, kittens and chickens wandering round her. She wasn't often still, and I thought we might not see her again. Then some sound in the field alerted her, and instantly she turned her head to it and

pricked her ears (as far up as they would ever go) – still on the job.

Then we returned home from a long journey to the Khyber and the Himalayas and found a surprising letter in the post, with a Welsh postmark. The signature, John Clough, was strange to us. The letter was clear and businesslike; he had heard the Thomases were building a bungalow down at Ffarmers, and as he thought Panteg farmhouse might be falling vacant, also the land we leased them, he and his wife would like to apply for it. All the relevant details followed.

We went down in laburnum time. At Panteg, no one was at home but Dinah, who greeted us ecstatically. She had never looked better. Her body was hard with muscle under a very thick coat. We went to Jennifer's mother for milk and eggs, but no one was there either. We saw the half-built bungalow nearby that would be Jennifer and Ivor's new home – not far from where she had been living in the caravan when we first met her.

Later that evening a car arrived at Gilfach'; Jennifer, her mother, her sister, and the two children. Her mother said, 'Someone saw your car leaving my farm, and thought maybe you'd come for milk and eggs, so we've brought you some.' Jennifer came in while Ralph stayed and chatted to the others, and we had a brief talk standing in the Big Room. She'd just got up from 'flu. 'How could you clean the house? You shouldn't have done.' 'Oh!' she laughed, 'The children helped me.'

I said I was sorry they were going, as I'd thought they were fond of the place. 'Oh, yes,' she said, 'but I felt if we didn't own our own home before we were too old, we never should.'

She had found her thirtieth birthday very traumatic the previous December. We were both Sagittarians, which was a link. I understood her driven urgency to do something – something different; to move, to move on: the panic that life was passing. She had been eight years on the mountain.

'What about Dinah?' I asked. Jennifer was very worried about that. 'I couldn't tie her up or shut her up, she'd hate it. And if I left her loose there beside the road she'd get run over. She's always been, so to speak, a free agent. Rather than have her unhappy, I'd have her put down.'

We went to see the Cloughs. It was pouring with rain that evening and the ground sodden. We made careful enquiries about where they lived – on the other side of Ffarmers – but it was one of those places you ask as you go. We set out with gumboots and a big torch in the car. On the road beyond Jennifer's mother we asked, as advised, at the last farm. A man in oilskins working on a tractor in the driving rain, gave clear and detailed instructions. 'You go along as far as you can, then the road stops. You go through a gate to your right, there's a track you should be able to drive.' He glanced doubtfully at our car. 'At the end of that there's another gate on your right. You can't drive any further. Leave the car and walk along the path between two fields; then you climb up the hill to the left. When you get up to the top, you should be able to see the roof of their house down in a little valley.'

All this we did, but as the rain was so heavy, and it was getting dark, Ralph was casting about like a game dog before he saw it. The chief problem was not to slip in the mud. Sheep looked at us in surprise. We came upon a van parked on the hillside with a ewe in the back. I could only see eyes glinting, she didn't move. We assumed it was the Cloughs' van, and that this was as near as they could get it to their house. Then round the curve of a hill we saw a little farm with outbuildings, and a faint light. We slithered muddily down to it.

They both came to the door. We'd met Sue because she worked opposite a garage we used, but we hadn't met John. They took our wet things, and lent us lovely snug carpet slippers, and we went in to a little room of firelight and lamplight. It was like arriving on board a boat in harbour after a rough passage – to come suddenly from the wild blackness outside into this cosy mellow calm.

When we had got acquainted with John, Sue, the sheep-dog Frank and the cat – I asked them to come and see us at Gilfachwen. I meant this as a signal to Ralph that in my opinion they were the right people to have Panteg.

They came on an evening as sunny and serene as the other had been black and stormy. We had a drink to our shared future, and when the business was concluded, Ralph took them up the hill to see a fencing problem, as they wanted to get their sheep on to our land as soon as possible. I saw their three figures silhouetted against the skyline; Ralph in his red sweater, and the two young people walking for the first time the fields that would be theirs.

Author's Note: For those interested in Dinah.

Jennifer had Dinah 'put down' before she left Panteg. She had the vet come to the house – not for her that selfish cruelty of sending an animal away to be killed among strangers. Dinah died in her own bed, the straw in the barn where she slept, and where, lately, she had spent a lot of the day. Jennifer was with her. Later, she buried her in the garden. 'I did that by myself,' she said. The first time we came down after this had happened, Ralph said to Jennifer, 'I feel she's still here, guarding the pass!' and Jennifer answered, 'Oh yes, I feel that very strongly, that she's still about.' Then she said a strange thing – strange for a girl accustomed to think of animals as something you earn your living by: 'It seems a funny thing to say; I know she was only an animal; but just at the end – she looked so proud!'

WILD WALES

ITS PEOPLE, LANGUAGE AND SCENERY

George Borrow

Wild Wales is a classic travel book, one that ranks with the work of Defoe or Cobbett. George Borrow immortalized the 'land of old renown and wonder, the land of Arthur and Merlin', the wild mountains, the green valleys, the tiny villages, the kindly, hospitable but mysterious people. Compiled by a great artist who understood and respected his subject, it describes landscapes and industrial works, mansions and cottages. Welsh heroes and poets have their high places, and even the people to be met with on the highway are rendered with astonishing vigour, for Borrow knew how to elevate a commonplace conversation and how to give it pathos and a new significance.

All Borrow's art, his insight, keenness of observation and feeling for human destiny, were used to give his readers an affectionate interpretation of the Welsh and their history. His own character and interests gave shape, as well as humour and directness, to a wholly delightful book. More than a hundred years after its first publication, *Wild Wales* remains the best book about Wales ever written.

Hammond Innes

'He is a master of suspense.' *Spectator*

Levkas Man £1.50
High adventure in Amsterdam, Malta and the Greek island of Levkas. 'Quick-action adventure—with a particularly interesting background'. *Daily Telegraph*

The Lonely Skier £1.50
'From the first page we are gripped by the sense of tension, mystery and urgency that Hammond Innes so well commands.' *Elizabeth Bowen*

Solomons Seal £1.75
A unique and priceless stamp is the violent legacy of a strange family to an ordinary Englishman. The result is a far-flung quest ending in the South Pacific where the murderous family vendetta, sun, sorcery and the copper-rich islands ripe for violence, combine to create an inescapable maelstrom.
  'Masterful storytelling, pace and precision'. *The Times*

North Star £1.50
A story of infiltration and sabotage in the North Sea aboard an oil rig. 'A master story-teller, at his best when the sea is one of the chief characters.' *Daily Telegraph*

FONTANA PAPERBACKS

Hammond Innes

'He is a master of suspense.' *Spectator*

Air Bridge £1.75
'Hammond Innes achieves a masterly sense of urgency as the story rises to the climax.' *Daily Telegraph*

Attack Alarm £1.35
Hammond Innes wrote this book 'under fire' as a young gunner during the Battle of Britain. 'Tightens suspense to the pitch of nightmare.' *L. A. G. Strong*

Campbell's Kingdom £1.65
'A fast and expertly-managed story... The Rockies, the squalid "ghost towns", the oil-boring— these are memorably presented.' *Sunday Times*

Golden Soak £1.75
Embittered and disillusioned with his life, Alec Falls fakes his own death and starts for Australia – and the Golden Soak mine. But he is not the only person interested in the derelict mine. The shadows of the past and the blistering hell of the Australian bush combine in a deadly maze which Falls must unravel if he is to survive at all...

'Pace, atmosphere, tension. Evokes Australia as few other books have done.' *Listener*

FONTANA PAPERBACKS

Fontana Paperbacks: Non-fiction

Fontana is a leading paperback publisher of non-fiction, both popular and academic. Below are some recent titles.

- ☐ THE POLITICS OF INDUSTRIAL RELATIONS (second edition) Colin Crouch £2·95
- ☐ NATTER NATTER Richard Briers £1·50
- ☐ KITCHEN HINTS Hilary Davies £1·25
- ☐ MRS WEBER'S DIARY Posy Simmonds £2·50
- ☐ A TREASURY OF CHRISTMAS Frank & Jamie Muir £2·95
- ☐ THE VIDEO HANDBOOK John Baxter & Brian Norris £1·95
- ☐ A BOOK OF SEA JOURNEYS Ludovic Kennedy (ed.) £3·50
- ☐ BEDSIDE GOLF Peter Alliss £1·95
- ☐ DAY CARE Alison Clarke-Stewart £1·95
- ☐ THE WOMAN QUESTION: READINGS ON THE SUBORDINATION OF WOMEN Mary Evans (ed.) £3·95
- ☐ WAR FACTS NOW Christy Campbell £2·50
- ☐ CHRONICLE OF YOUTH Vera Brittain £2·75
- ☐ FRIGHTENED FOR MY LIFE Geoff Coggan & Martin Walker £1·95
- ☐ HIGH PRESSURE: WORKING LIVES OF WOMEN MANAGERS Cary Cooper & Marilyn Davidson £1·95
- ☐ TRADE UNIONS: THE LOGIC OF COLLECTIVE ACTION Colin Crouch £2·50
- ☐ THE KINGDOM Robert Lacey £2·95
- ☐ A FOREIGN FLAVOUR Rose Elliot £2·95
- ☐ SEVEN DAYS TO DISASTER Des Hickey & Gus Smith £2·50
- ☐ P.S. I LOVE YOU Michael Sellers £1·75

You can buy Fontana paperbacks at your local bookshop or newsagent. Or you can order them from Fontana Paperbacks, Cash Sales Department, Box 29, Douglas, Isle of Man. Please send a cheque, postal or money order (not currency) worth the purchase price plus 10p per book (or plus 12p per book if outside the UK).

NAME (Block letters) _____

ADDRESS _____

_____

_____